FUTURE

LIFE

PROGRESSION

MEETING YOUR
FUTURE SELF

ZORANANDA GLAMOCLIJA

Future Life Progression
Copyright © 2020 by Zorananda Glamoclija

Tellwell Talent
www.tellwell.ca

ISBN
978-0-2288-3275-1 (Hardcover)
978-0-2288-3274-4 (Paperback)
978-0-2288-3276-8 (eBook)

TABLE OF CONTENTS

Acknowledgement...v

Introduction.. vii

Part 1

Chapter 1.   Re-Cognition... 3

Chapter 2.   Repetition 14

Chapter 3.   Merging.. 30

Part 2

Chapter 4.   Retrieval 47

Chapter 5.   Acceleration 67

Chapter 6.   Futurist Perspective...................................... 76

Part 3

Chapter 7.   Mystical Rhythms 93

Chapter 8.   The Microdosing Body 130

About the Author...141

Bibliography..145

ACKNOWLEDGEMENT

O ver the course of writing this book, many things have changed. Many people have come and gone, yet the spirit of Future Life Progression (FLP) has undoubtedly remained. My family has always been there to support me and will continue to support me. Out of everyone who has experienced FLP, one dear friend has helped immensely. Thank you, Tessa, for believing in this project and seeing it through to the end. Your hard work on the first round of editing and contribution to clarifying the concepts has enriched this book more than I could have ever hoped to do on my own.

To my dear Alicia, my soul mate and life partner, thank you for witnessing this book's birth and listening to my thoughts, fears, joys, and everything in between. Your patience and belief in me have helped maintain the momentum and inspiration I needed to write the final word.

To the reader of this book, thank you for taking the first step toward a deeper connection with your heart and a new-found relationship with your future self. May this book be of great help and encouragement for you! Follow the call of your heart and the synchronicities will guide you along harmoniously.

INTRODUCTION

The future is a vague hope veiled by the taboo beliefs that anything further than one to five years is impossible to know. In a manner of speaking, imagining where one will end up in the distant future takes one away from one's current life and deludes the mind from what is in the present. "Be in the now," is echoed far and wide, leaving dreamers bewildered by any natural inclination to become something more than what is currently inhabiting the now. The past is known and recollected as the experiences that have shaped the person and identity presently living and breathing. A picture of the past is framed in every household with the statement, "That's me... when I was five," and how true it sounds, how true it feels. The picture comes to life as the memory vividly plays in the mind, showcasing the child and their life as a five-year-old. "I remember that day! My mom took this picture right before my first day of school." Reinforced and rejoiced, the child and the person are now one and the same. The memory flees and the mind is left blank; the child suddenly gone, returned to the past, or so it seems. In place of that child is a person in a developed form carved by experience and environment, no longer innocent and naive to the world at large. However, though the person is no longer a child, a quality remains: internal blindness to the future and what it may hold.

The continual development of life through time is shaped by three aspects that are comfortably spoken about regularly, yet undermined for the sake of convenience. Our inner world and its capacity can represent an expansive reserve allowing for organization and expression of the past, present, and future. Reality is the tangible hardness and physicality that can be rightly experienced presently and lucidly without any extra internal force. Why look toward the further reaches of the future to imagine something that may not happen when one can grab a book off the shelf and read it now? The past is gone and done with, so why try to investigate whether physical and emotional ailments are symptoms of past traumas? It seems the past is only good for pleasant memories and the *remember-that-one-time-when*, and the future to the extent of the next planned week-long vacation. The traumatic past is tainted by grief, and the farther future of purpose is veiled by anxiety and doubt—the present marks the only place where any pleasure can occur, truly.

The past, present, and future extend endlessly while one life is marked by birth and death in a period with no resemblance to any kind of endlessness. However, the prospect of feeling there is something more that may not be reached physically but can be reached mentally and spiritually endures. I hope to unveil that the past, present, and future can be greatly influenced and affected by the personal intention of contact, more so a spiritual intention of contact. By contact, I mean communication and observation. When recalling the past, we normally conclude that nothing can be done to change what had happened. Regarding the future, we usually conclude that it is too uncertain to know what we hope to occur will indeed occur.

The first three sections of this introduction will explore the three versions of the self I have identified throughout my practice. FIrstly, we will delve into the future and how the collective of humanity has shaped the idea that the distant future is unknowable; secondly, the present and the embodiment of life as a human being; and lastly, the past to explore the timeline and development of Future Life Progression.

The Future

As each day passes by, the perceivable future is relative to the effort one makes toward achieving life goals. However, at times, it seems that regardless of effort, the future is ambiguous as spontaneous unforeseen events interrupt the flow of routine. An unsavory discouragement endorses the doubtful belief that it is futile to have any control of the future. Limitations remind each of us of our insignificance; all that is necessary is the day by day simplicity and manageable escapes from the mundane through vacations and holidays, to alcohol and substance use. Why is there a limit to the internal visual scope of observing life goals that are more distant in the future?

A good friend, Joshua Beeler, once explained to me his experience and process of envisioning the distant future. He's a planner, and he's good at it. Although he can create a successful progression of events a year at a time, there is a point where beyond a year or two, something happens:

> *"Occasionally, perhaps every two years, there is an event that I know will happen, yet beyond which I cannot see any further into the future. In the past, the event has been something like the completion and release of a software project or going to Burning Man. Events like these hang in front of me like a black curtain. I can see and plan into the future up to such an event, but I cannot see or plan beyond it. I seem to predict how the event will resolve and how that will change my circumstances on the other side of the black curtain. I just have to wait until the event is closer to the present, is happening, or comes to pass to see what's on the other side of the curtain."*

The result for him is a sudden pierce of anxiety due to the uncertainty. Any attempt to approach the curtain and peek through amplifies the anxiety. Inevitably, for my friend, the curtain remains darkened to only be opened when the *appropriate* time comes to unveil what the future beholds.

Typically, the future is approached rationally. Through logical reasoning, events are considered, and each scenario of possibility is weighed until a "sound" potential reality is envisioned. With reasoning comes feeling. An intuitive undercurrent subtly suggests whether the imagined future is feasible or otherwise more fantasy than reality. Often, logical reasoning gains a much louder voice than the subtle, suggestive feeling of intuition; however, such reasoning only goes so far. This is due to biases around the desired future. The picture of what will happen seems impossible to know or witness, as the biases uphold beliefs that favor certain outcomes. If logical reasoning is a biased viewing of the potential future, then intuition is the *mechanism* for experiencing the picture of the future.

In my friend's situation, logical reasoning works for his daily, weekly, and monthly life planning, developed through his learned ability to manage his general livelihood and life goals. If there is anything beyond what he can fathom, anxiety prevents any logical ability to see beyond the curtain. All the while, intuition is in the current moment and far into the future, indicating that logic is a compartmentalization of the whole picture that arises from intuition.

The future is potential, at least in terms of societal normality. Generally, the *collective hive mind* that makes up humanity agrees that there are limits to viewing the unknown future. However, there are spontaneous and seemingly random occurrences that raise curiosity for those who have prophetic visions and dreams. Yet, the hive mind of the collective consciousness is an immovable sphere of influence when it comes to specific beliefs and ideologies. When individual cases emerge to suggest the distant future can be certain, viewed, and interacted with, the hive mind secures its foundational belief that anything about the distant future is a fallacy. This is similar to the louder voice of reasoning that drowns out the subtle suggestions of intuition within an individual. Where do these beliefs come from? What is being hindered in the process of adopting the societal accepted belief that the distant future is uncertain?

The Present

Right now, I am seated at a desk in a Shanghai hotel awaiting my next flight to Rishikesh, India, where I will spend the next month in the Anand Prakash Ashram to assist in a two-hundred-hour teacher training. So, the prior scenario is a glimpse of the past, and includes a small detail about the future. However, everything that has just been said happened in the present, all without causing mental strain on any capacity to think about the past, present, and future. There is a capacity to know how far-reaching the past and future extend. That capacity is dependent on developmental factors through meditative effort and is only available in the present moment. Is it simply enough to say that it is impossible to know clear and precise details of the past and future? I would wager that it is impossible only because of personal capacity. At this very moment, there can be a very liberating opportunity to realize, "I can use the mind however I wish."

Concerning the past and future, currently, we are all capable of diving into memories to recollect moments and into the *imagination* to conjure what experiences we would like happen in the future. Just as the mind had suddenly expanded outwards into the ethers of itself, it retracts/contracts back to where you are physically taking up space. The duration of time between the expansion into farther reaches of the future and retraction back to the present can be lengthened by continual meditative effort. Thus, it is the development of capacity in the meditative effort, which allows for the time spent internally exploring the past and future to lengthen. Without the meditative effort, the retraction will occur spontaneously on its own, resulting in conclusive remarks about impossibility. Perhaps, when asked about future plans, you have heard a friend mention one of the following comments. "It's impossible to know what my life will be like in ten years. I can't even consider what's going to happen a month from now!" Because the future includes infinite potential and possibility, the retraction back to the present moment occurs much sooner than when exploring the past. That is because of experience. The past has content, context, and recognizable personal features, while the future does not. When pondering the future, the content and context must be supplied by the person, which can be tiresome mentally. The past is like a movie, and you are the viewer. Concerning the future, you become the writer, director, and producer. The memories from the past have a character who has developed into you. The future? It has a character as well, and currently, you don't know how the development will occur. It seems no matter how much any of us fantasize and daydream, that character seems completely unreal. So, what's missing? *Feeling.* The past seems real because how we felt, can be remembered. When it comes to the future, we can't feel what the future self is feeling. We only know how we once felt and how we feel now. Through personal development, we can assess how life will shift to some degree in the future. Can there be a process which identifies how the future self feels in *their* present moment?

The Past: Inception

As a child, I had regularly pondered and daydreamed about the future. A natural curiosity allowed me to slip away from the physical world into a grey haze of flashing visions twisted by fantasy and desire. Being born to lower/middle class immigrant parents, there was a part of me that understood these fantastic desires wouldn't truly occur, yet I continued to slip away and tell myself I would become a professional soccer player, skateboarder, snowboarder, or whatever I obsessed over at the time. Though I enjoyed fabricating all kinds of scenarios in my mind, not all were of my doing. Some I had intercepted, as if placed within the mind mysteriously as a spectacle to witness rather than create.

One impactful experience I remember occurred when I was eight years old. I had been walking home from school, taking the route home I was accustomed to. It was an ordinary day. The neighborhood was quiet, the sky was slightly overcast, and it was in the middle of spring. The route I would take every day was along a road that led to the townhomes I grew up in. Before the townhomes begin, there is a horseshoe of houses to the right and two small apartment buildings to the left, followed by a small outlet mall of a few stores. There is an alleyway that divides the houses from the town-homes perpendicular to the stores, and between the last house and the alley is a white fence. As I walked by the houses, daydreaming about all sorts of things, a vision suddenly arose in my mind in such a way that everything around me disappeared yet remained. I saw a scene of myself walking up to the alley's entrance and getting hit by a large white truck. As I saw myself in this collision, I abruptly returned to myself and stopped right before the alley. At that very moment, a white truck stopped suddenly, screeching its brakes. After I gave the truck a perplexed and shocked look, I ran home as fast as possible!

Over the years of my adolescence, I had forgotten about the white truck. It wasn't until later in my teens I recollected the vision and began considering what truly occurred. I had been pondering time travel around then, differently, of course, to any techno-scientific vein of consideration. There was a synchronicity between my new-found curiosity that we could travel through time *internally* and the memory of my near-death experience at the age of eight. It all made sense within my young mind. Why would we need a machine to travel through time? We hop daily into the past and dream about the future equally as much. However, I wanted to know how it could be done tangibly as a physical experience likened to the present moment. And like any teenager approaching young adulthood, distractions of life continued to push away the curiosity for more engaging rituals of friendships and lively outings.

As maturity sculpted my mind, the synchronicities brought an abundance of experiences to further my understanding of the expansive properties of the past, present, and future. I began to yearn for the knowledge and information that my own pondering and curiosity could not supply. A discourse of inner work was needed to allow me to more willfully delve into understanding how I managed to have that vision at eight years old without having created it myself. Thus, a long scouring of the internet began.

By the age of eighteen, I had found years' worth of information ranging from spiritual to metaphysical, to occult teachings and beyond. What I stumbled upon that pointed directly toward knowing more deeply about my experience at eight years old was concepts and case studies of contact with the higher self. I had learned about a couple of individuals who had been under hypnosis when their higher self came through, taking over and telling the hypnotist about the person under hypnosis. There was one story that intrigued me. A boy in the U.S had been deathly allergic to all types of flowers and plants to the extent he could barely be outside. When all options were exhausted, he was sent to a psychologist who practiced hypnotherapy. Upon being hypnotized, the boy's voice changed as he began to speak. The voice then explained that it was the child's higher self. Taken aback, the psychologist asked why it had come through, and the higher self explained that it had known about the psychologist's attempts to learn about the boy's allergies. The higher self explained that the boy had been a wealthy man in his most recent past life. When the wealthy man retired, he became obsessed with his garden. The man had everything he ever needed, and therefore, never left his mansion. When the man eventually passed on, a condition was set in place that he would manifest as a boy with severe allergies to learn his lesson about isolation and obsession in the next life. After hearing the story, the psychologist had asked the higher self if the boy had learned his lesson. The higher self confirmed he had and then departed, bringing the boy back without the psychologist commanding so. The child was confused, as he had no memory of the experience. The psychologist then went to the far side of the room to a newly pollinating flower, brushed some pollen onto her hand, then sat next to the boy and lightly blew the pollen into his face. The boy was aghast! He let out a scream, but the therapist asked him to breathe. To the boy's surprise, he could breathe clearly and had no allergic reaction! After reading this incredible case, I wondered whether I could meet my higher self through hypnosis.

Nearly a year after I had read this case, I continued to contemplate the reality of contacting a higher self. I began to search for local hypnotherapists that could help facilitate the process. After a somewhat lengthy search, I came upon a man named Padman Pillai. He was an elderly Indian man with extensive experience in hypnosis. Upon seeing his picture on the internet, I knew he would be the one to help me. When I spoke with him to set up a session, we talked about the different reasons for hypnosis, and I told him I was more interested in past life regression as I felt it would be the route to take, given the case about the boy. However, I didn't tell him about my intention. I let it be that I was curious to learn about my past life.

It was just after my birthday in November when I ventured to meet Padman. He had his office set up in the basement of his home. It was not a typical bi-level split basement. Padman had created a sacred and welcoming space for his work, including vaulted raised ceilings and a walk-out patio that invited the sun to stream gently onto his office floor. After warm introductions and an explanation of the process of his type of hypnosis, we began the work. Soft music was playing in the background as I reclined onto a comfortable chocolate toned couch. I could tell this couch was specially selected to host these kinds of experiences. He began to guide me through the beginning process of relaxing my body and calming my mind. Slowly and gently, he guided me through the darkness of my mind to the subconscious.

With Padman's guidance, I came to a door that was illuminated around its seams. As I reached to open the door, the illuminating light poured through and surrounded me. On the other side of the door, I stepped into the center of a round plaza in a small, quiet town. Strangely, I was alone. Beyond the plaza was a scene of open sky, mountain foothills, and a castle to the left in the distance. I looked down at my hands and body and noticed I was still a man. In front of me was a fountain with a statue in the middle, and shops lining the plaza's perimeter. There was a road that led out of the town center toward the castle, dipping down into the valley of the countryside. The houses that ran along the road slowly spaced further apart as it tracked into the distance.

When Padman began to ask me what I was seeing and who I was, sudden flashes of memories flooded into my past life. I had been a soldier for the king. Though I was a commoner, I had gained the king's respect because of my chivalry and honor as a soldier. I had been a part of his close guard until the church was built. At that time, churches had entered kingdoms through factions who claimed to be representatives of God and wanted to help steer the kingdoms into the direction of holy union. Shortly after the church was completed, my position had been replaced by the soldiers the church had provided. Many men in the town and countryside had been put out of work, yet forced to pay newly raised taxes.

I was an angry man. I found myself unable to quell my monstrous rage and anger toward the church. That rage was only subdued in one instance: Padman had asked me if I could see anyone else in the past life, perhaps someone close to me. I was outside of my home and turned around to see the most beautiful and magnificent woman, and I felt an immense love and joy. The feeling was an overwhelming surge that took my breath away. A great light emanated from the woman. In a high shrill voice, I said, "It's my wife!" We had a beautiful daughter together, and I felt a great tenderness for her.

As though on a roller coaster, I felt an abrupt plummet again into anger and rage, and I suddenly found myself in a dimly lit room full of men. It was well past midnight. We were discussing the corruption and manipulation that had occurred since the church had come. The king had been usurped without even knowing it. We were his old guards and soldiers, and I had invited them to meet in secrecy to plan a coup. However, it was grounded in justice, with evidence showing the church had been siphoning money from the king with their new banking system. This time, the rage and anger felt good. I was around men whom I trusted and who equally felt such anger. The boiling rage strengthened our spirits. My best friend was beside me in the cellar. I remember looking in his eyes and feeling we had everything we needed to win. My friend was a newly appointed guard for the church and therefore knew the church and daily guard shifts well. What I didn't realize was that my best friend had been manipulated to uproot us. Before we could execute our plan, the church began seeking us out one at a time for extermination.

The passing of time wasn't so straight forward in the past life, neither in Padman's office. What seemed like years in the past life was minutes in our reality. It was midday when the church guards came to my door. I was frantic. My wife and child were missing, and it didn't take long to realize my best friend had betrayed me. The guards barged in and, without hesitation, brought my life to an end. My present self hadn't even flinched at the sight of the violent death of my past self. Silently and gently, I began to drift away from my body. I was floating to the top of the room. When I turned to look behind me, my past life was gone. In its place was an intense blinding light. I gazed into the light silently. I wondered if the light was only blinding because I was staring directly into it. I shifted into peripheral vision and beheld seven beings standing, emanating from the light that had taken over my past life.

Padman suddenly asked me what was happening. I hadn't realized that I'd become silent. My past life came back in a flash. Trying not to lose what I was currently experiencing in the hypnosis, I explained to him that I had died by the sword of a guard, and they had taken my body from my home. Involuntarily, the brilliant light came flooding in again. Unaware of Padman's office and the session, I stood face to face with the seven beings. On the far left, one of them pointed at me and said, "You are one of us standing here." Padman again asked what was happening, a bit agitated that I was not communicating with him. However, I cut him off and said, "That is not important. There are seven beings of light standing before me, and one said I am one of them. They are the masters of cycles." Padman snapped his fingers and, with it, brought the whole experience to an end. I came to and did not feel relaxed. I was completely stiff and vibrating, which left me out of breath and exhausted. I asked him why he brought me out. He paused for a moment, then gently said, "In my twenty-five years of hypnosis, I have never had this experience. I didn't want anything to happen to you. It's best that I brought you back."

We ended the session there. Though startled, Padman was grateful for our hypnosis session. On that chilly November evening, as I walked out of his home, the night sky was illuminated by a brilliant full moon. I smiled and recollected the seven beings. I knew that at that moment, my life was forever changed.

Many years went by, and my life had indeed changed. Yoga became a dominant fixture in my daily routine. Though I had begun focusing on life as a businessman, the deep desire for mystical and esoteric knowledge had remained. Through synchronicity, I had been led to ponder and contemplate the future's influence on the present moment, mainly that our insights and inspirations come from our future self. In the beginning, these thoughts perplexed me. I began to yearn for something to show me that my thoughts and insights were real. I hadn't any more experiences in that way for some time until one specific morning that marked my journey of creating Future Life Progression (FLP).

Upon waking, I gently remained in that space between dreaming and waking; that silent darkness that ebbs between the two. As I was enjoying the serenity of the void, I suddenly saw my face. It was noticeably different. My hair was peppered with grey and white and tied up in a pony-tail. My face appeared content yet solemn. I will always remember the eyes; they were relaxed and fixed, gazing deeply. Then I heard a voice say, "Are you ready to continue?" I agreed, and the face disappeared. A flood of emotion had taken the place of the vision's face, and I knew that at that moment, everything I had gone through had come to a precipice. This was my calling to create a meditation to contact the future self.

Nearly a year had gone by after seeing the face of my future self. During that year, I recollected everything I had learned regarding the past, present, and future. Flashes of my childhood and little wonderings danced across my mind, serene moments spent at a yoga school in Thailand reminded me of teachings that reaffirmed insights and realizations, and current synchronicities initiated the process to begin offering FLP. The most significant synchronicity to have come my way was a beautiful three-story historical home that housed six incredible friends. It was in this house affectionately dubbed "Sunbelly" that I had begun FLP as a monthly meditation. In October of that year, I had moved into Sunbelly and thought it befitting to have the first FLP meditation on my birthday the following November. It would be a day to mark the birth of FLP, just as it marked my own.

FLP had begun to grow and attract an inspiring group of twelve individuals who returned month after month to learn more about their future selves. Each month, I became increasingly more creative concerning new content to deepen the process for us all. Little did I know that creativity had served a personal purpose. In the summer of 2016, I had a wonderful experience during my morning meditation. It was a Sunday morning. I had done a small yoga and meditation practice before attending a kundalini class with my childhood friend Kris Elaschuk. As I sat silently, expanding my attention and focus into my heart, an image flashed before me. The background was black, and the image sharp and vivid. A woman wearing a royal blue sparkling slender gown, with short white hair, was sitting on a throne. With her eyes wide yet happy and a small curious smile on her lips, words began to fill the dark space of my mind, "You know who I am. You named your harp after me. More importantly, I am you." Without any time to respond, the woman vanished, and I sat alone in silence. A shiver crawled across me, and I looked over at my harp across the living room... *Amareld*.

I recalled the image as often as I could on my way to and during Kris' kundalini class. The excitement within me was pulsating. I hadn't had an experience like that since I saw my aged face that one morning, but to see someone else so clearly and interact in a way where I wasn't in control of the dialogue or vision was beyond exceptional! After the kundalini class, I remained in the studio to meditate silently. Naturally, I began slipping into the expansive space within my heart. The soothing depth of silence and pulsing tenderness suddenly brought me to a room that looked like a cathedral. The ceilings soared nearly fifty feet high, and the room itself a hundred feet long. Glowing stained glass windows raised from the floor to ceiling, covering the expanse of the room on both sides and painting it in gentle hues of various colors as the light from outside filtered through. Focusing in front of me, my heart was suddenly gripped in anticipation. Amareld sat on a throne at the opposite end. In what would seem like an impossible manner, one step brought me to the foot of her throne.

"I have been waiting for you for a long time," she gently spoke with her curious smile, "I am you, as you are me." She was gazing deeply into my eyes.

"You are my future self?" I asked.

"Yes. I am you, 538 years in the future."

I was astonished. Here I was, fully embr
my future self.

"Remember your vision of the white tr
Amareld asked. I confirmed, and she cont'
timeologists, I had sent that vision to you when I was a ս—
safety and life are important to us. We can only do this work because ս—
you and FLP. It will become more than what you know it as now." As she
spoke, she showed me her memories of being a small child working with
the timeologists. I saw within the memory the moment she had sent me
the future vision that saved my life. Tears began to form in my eyes. "You
must continue with Future Life Progression," were her last words before
I returned to my body. It seemed like hours had passed, yet the entire
interaction happened within minutes. With glassy eyes and a smile on my
face, I stood up with a strong feeling of purpose and a new determination
to further the creation of FLP.

Future Life Progression: Conception

Over the years, FLP had shifted and changed. Year after year, I introduced
new techniques to improve the process of contacting one's future self. FLP
took many years to perfect through trial and error, and in my opinion, the
first two years were incomplete. It was in the third year that a significant
shift had occurred to create a whole new system. A seed had been planted
after the experience I had with Amareld, and the realization had grown into
a conscious idea while I was completing a three-hundred-hour Akhanda
Yoga teacher training in Rishikesh, India.

The yoga teacher training was more than just training. It had provided
me the opportunity and time to begin formulating FLP as a precise
methodology. FLP needed a foundation and framework that would be
as unique as a process. How that process could be conceived needed
additional inspiration. Before the training, I had come across a book with
my childhood friend Kris. We were perusing the small "used" section of a
bookstore one afternoon when he immediately came to me and said, "You
have to get this book! You won't find it anywhere else. I'm actually surprised

the used book section, no less!" That book was *Kaballah and of Dreaming* by Catherine Shainberg. Kris had spoken to me Catherine and her work many times in the past. Finding her book day wasn't random. Kris was meant to find it, and I was meant to read it. I began reading it on my way to India and completed it during my time in the training. What I had learned from Catherine's work helped me form the kind of foundation FLP needed. However, *Kaballah and the Power of Dreaming* was not the sole source of inspiration that shaped what FLP is today. Some time had passed upon returning from India, and I had already begun formulating the structure of FLP. I sought out the book store where I had found Catherine's book, and another one caught my attention. The second source of inspiration came from *The Path of the Dreamhealer* by Adam Mcleod. As I read through his book, many insights that I had already written were confirmed and reconfirmed. Every day that I spent creating the new sequence of FLP, Adam's book would confirm nearly every insight. I spent most of 2017 working out each section of the sequence, referencing Catherine and Adam's books to find correlations with what insights had arisen within me. *Meeting Your Future Self* had finally taken shape in eight steps:

1. Re-cognition
2. Repetition
3. Merging
4. Retrieval
5. Acceleration
6. Futurist Perspective
7. Mystical Rhythms
8. The Microdosing Body

Thus, FLP is the exercises, processes, and necessary information to prepare for meeting your future self. The two meditations that prepare for the encounter and connection with the future self are:

1. Heart Awareness Meditation
2. Dream Awareness Meditation

At this point, it is important to know and comprehend a crucial lesser-known fact concerning time. The past, present, and future occur in one single duration. Our relationship with time is closely entwined with physical reality, and, as such, it is viewed linearly. However—and this may be a bold statement—consciousness itself, as a universal property, allows the past, present, and future to occur in one moment simultaneously in their own frame of experiences. Although pragmatically and logically, it is unfeasible to experience all three aspects of time in one duration physically, there is, however, a function within humanity that has direct access to time in a realm that is nonphysical and non-linear, where all moments of time are frozen in still frames. That function will be thoroughly explained throughout this book as Future Life Progression – Meeting Your Future Self.

The process of FLP is intuitive and simple. Though there are complexities in each step of FLP, the key to easily comprehending the nature of time, the ability to heal the past, and the journey toward communicating with your future self is sharing consciousness with the heart's process of decision making. Just as we are currently in a physical realm that hosts space in three dimensions, there is a paralleling nonphysical realm that hosts time in three dimensions, and the heart functions in both realms. It is a lesser-known fact that before a decision is made, the heart has already processed what you will choose before the brain strives to act on it. The information the heart picks up before the brain comes from that nonphysical realm and is sent to the brain to be actualized in the physical realm. In the physical realm, time can only and naturally be viewed as a gradual unfolding from moment to moment, blended together by the direct experience of physicality. In the nonphysical realm, time can be viewed entirely as an empty space that is unmoving yet filled with snapshots of events that come to life when focused upon. It is in that realm your future self can be experienced. Through the process of FLP, you will discover a door within your heart that leads to the nonphysical time realm. In that realm, the guided meditations in this book will inspire healing of the past and welcome your future self. Close your eyes and imagine meeting your future self who is wise, loving, and deeply caring for you and your harmonious impact in the world.

The benefit of FLP is a communication with a future self that has a memory of all the events and decisions that you will eventually experience. The advantage and opportunity you will receive is navigation through life with guidance and support from your future self, who exists in the life you are striving toward. The more you connect to your future self through FLP, the more knowledge you will receive from your future self to create the harmoniously abundant life you deeply desire. Over the years of practicing and developing FLP, I have seen a wonderful manifestation of outcomes and experiences that have further amplified my creativity, courage, and curiosity. With every moment spent communicating with my future self, an abundance of insight and creativity flows into my world. Writing this book is one example of what can come from communicating with your future self. Creating your life in alignment with your heart, abundant with creativity, is my wish for everyone reading this book.

PART 1

CHAPTER 1

Re-Cognition

B efore waking, a transition occurs—a space of void that is neither dream state nor waking state. Slowly, the reality of the waking state solidifies, and the space of void is filled. The day's first thoughts arise and guide attention to the responsibilities that are to be acted upon. The dream before the space of void is sometimes recollected and sometimes forgotten as the vivid waking state takes hold of the body and its functions. The eyes open, and the body moves, ready to put forth action to begin the daily routine.

While it may not be so prominent as a unique experience, some of the first actions coming from a dream state is a "speaking" that occurs within the mind. Such speaking isn't without purpose. At times, this inner monologue is indeed intentional. Typically, however, it is initiated involuntarily in either circumstance; speaking within the mind upon waking activates specific parts of the brain. As a note, this book is not about neuroscience or an in-depth examination of total brain function. What information I provide is the reasoning for the step-by-step process of FLP. The part of the brain we will examine right now is the role and general function of the left hemisphere.

The left hemisphere of the brain is responsible for mundane to complex daily functions. The degree between the mundane and the complex changes from task to task and person to person, and shifts between functions such as logic, reason, writing, math, and language. Let's examine how the left brain interacts with a function such as language. Nearly everyone communicates using a language of sorts, from signing with their hands to verbal language from the glocal lexicon. Regardless of which language one uses, the left brain is involved. That involvement is utilized every day. From the moment we wake up to the moment we drift off to sleep, it plays a fairly dominant role. Decisions, conversations, and thoughts are encoded by whatever language we had been raised on. Language is so engrossed within our expression that nuances occur without our control. Song lyrics will play on repeat, and redundantly with annoyance, arguments with a friend will echo as we reframe our response, again and again, to rationalize what we had said until anger and frustration become overwhelming. Simply put, the left brain will *not* shut up.

During meditation, the steady stream of internal verbalization becomes strikingly pronounced. Right now, try to sit quietly without anything in your mind for one minute. Without any kind of preparation, technique, or experience, you will notice that quieting the mind deliberately—even for one minute—is seemingly impossible. There is a noticeable loop that can be observed. Like clockwork, by simply closing your eyes and intentionally not thinking verbal thoughts, a different phrase will appear every several seconds. Yet, is that all the left brain can do? Can its constant chatter be neutralized so its other unknown purposes can be utilized?

Generally, what we know of the right brain is of its creative capacity. Music, art, images, and spontaneity are associated with the right hemisphere of the brain. By spontaneity, I mean the out of nowhere creativity that arises at precise uncalculated moments. In the scientific community, it is well known that the right brain acts as a mapping system for the environment. Without putting any conscious effort into thinking about it, the right brain gathers information from all directions. Out of all the ways the right brain can express the totality of the information it receives, let's look at images.

Like the left hemisphere's constant chatter, the right brain also never ceases processing. However, the right hemisphere does much of its work in a way we don't consciously give attention to. This means there are images taken of the entire environment, frame by frame, and captured through all the senses. Because our primary focus is on the external world, the images captured by the right brain are kept internal. From time to time, for a split moment, we get a flash of a frame bright enough to grab our attention away from the external world and into the internal world. Typically, those flash frames are considered insignificant due to the impermanence and dissipating duration of the image. Remember the story of my experience of the white truck? That entire "vision" happened in a flash, yet, it was potent and vivid enough for me to take notice and stop to wonder about it. If I hadn't stopped to consider what I saw, I'm sure I would have been hit by the truck! These kinds of flash frame images occur every day all day. Their content, however, differs from moment to moment. The image may contain information from the past, present, or future. Why is it that we seem to filter these consistently occurring images out of our conscious thought unless they are particularly striking?

It is important to consider that the right brain does not operate through verbal language. Though we may be inspired by a painting or a piece of music to write poetry, the right brain has no part in formulating what is to be said about what is witnessed or heard. Why is this important? It can indicate how dominant the left brain is. Its dominance shows up through thinking. It is seemingly much easier to converse within the brain with language than it is with images. Try expressing this sentence with only images, "The blue chair in the solarium was covered in green and red vines that crawled along the tiled floor and down the stairs into the study room." While reading this sentence, the images jump out. Now take a moment to envision that entire scenario without those words. You may notice it takes conscious effort not to use the words above and simply see the image in your mind. This results from the left brain taking the dominant role by default and attempting to envision what only the right brain has spatial awareness to imagine. However, when we put words to the description, the left brain is preoccupied with the verbalization, allowing the right brain to pick up and create the images where the left brain cannot. The dominance of the left brain is such that the right, without training, will only vividly show the images when it is operating in tandem with the left hemisphere. Otherwise, the right brain will only show vivid images spontaneously without conscious direction. Therefore, it seems that we are dealing with conscious and subconscious tendencies. In this book, I will associate left brain activity with consciousness and right brain activity with subconsciousness. Why? Because we operate consciously, and the main proponent of our daily activities is geared by the left brain. Thus, the right brain is subconscious because its function is out of the scope of command and control. There is no direct deliberate control of the environmental mapping that occurs or the random images and visions that arise for the left brain to interpret.

How do the left and right brain hemispheres work together? The amount of information the right brain gathers is far greater than the left brain can handle. Just try to imagine processing all information in just one room logically. Not only would you have to consider all the objects you see in front of you, but the objects out of view as well. Along with all the objects, sounds, smells, and tactile feelings, the right brain categorizes all this information. This is very overwhelming for the left brain, so its job is to compartmentalize. It takes on what is necessary for conscious processing, hence the 120-degree vision that allows for the percentile of visual stimulation, perceivable hertz for auditory stimulation, and sensory sensitivity through touch. Imagine that the information gathered by the right brain is a pie. The left brain will take a slice of that pie required for necessary engagement in the environment. That slice of pie is only relevant to what the left brain identifies with, and the contents of that pie slice appeal to the left brain's sense of personality and behavioral patterns. While the left brain is geared on preference, the right brain is not.

Can the left brain be neutralized? What does that mean? With respect to the information in this book, this question explores whether the conscious and subconscious roles of the left and right brain hemispheres can be reversed. Can the left brain take on a subconscious role of operation, and the right brain take on a conscious role? Yes, they certainly can. However, the function of the left and right brain hemispheres change. That change can be attributed to an added component that is missing in our day to day decision making.

Process of Re-cognition

Here, the definition of "recognition" differs from what you'll find in a dictionary. *Re-cognition* deals with the process of neutralizing the left-brain hemisphere to allow for the right brain hemisphere to assume a more dominant role of utilization. Since using the left brain in a conscious logical manner is to cognize, using the right brain in a conscious intuitive manner is to re-cognize. Thus, through the initial re-cognition process, one construes the latent function after reversing the roles of left and right brain hemispheres.

In the following section of this chapter, we will explore an exercise that can indicate just how dominant the left brain is, help begin the process of neutralizing the dominance of the left brain, and unveil the power within the heart to initiate and maintain the role reversal between the left and right hemispheres.

Read through the exercise once. Come back to this point when you are done and take a few slow, deep breaths and then begin to imagine the scenario below with your eyes closed. You may already start to visualize or have ideas come to mind during your first reading as your right brain processes the words your left brain is interpreting. That is normal, and you are welcome to expand on those ideas and images once you begin to move through the meditation with your eyes closed. If you forget how the meditation moves forward, it is OK to open your eyes and quickly scan the paragraph below to find your pace. You may also consider recording the paragraph below at a slow pace and using your voice as a guide.

Once your eyes are closed, allow the blackness that comes to be the focus of your attention. In this blackness, allow for a troubling scenario to arise. This scenario can be a recollection of a past event, an argument you've had recently with a loved one, or a belief that inspires despair of the world. Allow the scenario to be as vivid as possible. Every breath breathes more and more life into what you are witnessing. Feel as emotions swirl around with the scenario. Immediately and spontaneously, imagine you have been watching that scenario through the end of a fiber optic cable. You see that the cable extends ahead of you into the blackness. Your hands appear in front of you. Take hold of the cable and begin pulling. You find that you are pulling yourself forward. As you move forward, you begin to feel that the cable is endless. The more you pull, the farther you move forward, while more and more cable appears. Immediately and spontaneously, realize your next pull brings you to the end. You see a box where the cable ends. You also see many more cable ends. As you look to your right and left, there are seemingly endless cable ends coming out of the box. Immediately and spontaneously, remove the cable completely out of the box.

Please do the guided meditation above before continuing...

After coming to the box and seeing the source of the cable, were you able to successfully pull the cable from the box? Did you imagine other ways to remove the cable? And when you saw more cables, did you remove them from the box as well? Was the exploration vivid? Did you notice that as you were moving through the blackness, pulling on the cable, that your mind was thoughtless? Did you notice that only the hand-over-hand action and forward movement was happening? Feel free to note these and any other observations in your journal.

This exercise is a stage of neutralizing the left brain. In the beginning, it needs the justification of control through interacting with the troubling scenario. The dialogue, movement, and feeling start to overwhelm the left brain, which brings on the more vivid experiences supplied by the right brain. The sudden shift to the blackness and fiber optic cable allows the right brain to take over more consciously. The left brain now plays a supportive role for the right brain to bring up spontaneous images to play out as a moving vision. However, the left brain isn't so docile. There will be moments of contortion and response to the experience. The cables will sway all over the place, little verbal responses will arise, and a realization of a never-ending cable will try and bring the brain back to its left-brain dominance. More focus on the forward movement will aid in applying more lucidity, and a different realization will occur. For instance, the realization can be created instantaneously in the end; thus, the troubling scenario appears. Because the right brain is much more dominant after the above exercise, the guidance to act does not come from a linguistic communication; rather, it is communication from intuition.

Intuition communicates through feeling and guides your attention through images, inspiring a feeling to act out the intuitive images. In the exercise, a few of you may have experienced the spontaneous decision to remove the other cables. This was intuitively known by felling the freedom that comes from no longer being affected by troubling thoughts and visions. Even though the scenarios of all the other cords attached to the box were unknown logically, it could have been known intuitively that releasing them would result in a noticeable feeling of relief. The continual practice and application is a sure way to conjure up the courage to remove the optic cable.

What did you notice after the short meditation? Was it clear and easy to follow? Or was it still a bit fuzzy and challenging to complete? Regardless of wherever the meditation went for you, the above exercise can be done at any time and yield a different experience each time. We are all unique in our own way of using imagination. New kinds of re-cognition exercises can arise spontaneously simply due to the more developed flowing lucidity through the right brain. To elaborate, the spontaneous nature of the right brain works with innate creative abilities to support the role reversal. As the right brain has become dominant, it still can spontaneously flash new images to inspire a deeper connection within the subconscious realm of the right brain. However, there is still an element missing. This element will securely maintain the role reversal and develop a greater capacity of knowing where the innate creativity is coming from.

Though the cable meditation is helpful, it is only one piece of the puzzle and still relies on the function of the left and right brain processes. The left brain is prepared for neutralization, and the right brain finally showcases its potent subconscious powers. However, the innate creativity I mentioned above arises through a meditative state induced by the heart. I have come to know this state as the "intelligence of the heart".

The heart's intelligence is a governing energy that powers the body, physical mind, and emotions. Everything on Earth has a heart, in one form or another. Every animal, insect, and plant utilizes a heart to supply their bodies with the necessities of life. The shape may change; however, the general and sophisticated functions remain. Without the heart, there would be no comprehension of life as we perceive it.

Regarding the human heart, its intelligence is a fully integrated mechanism that bridges the physical realms of experience to the spiritual nonphysical realms. Therefore, the cable meditation without the meditative state of the heart's intelligence can only work on the physical levels of the body, mind, and emotions. A method must be utilized beforehand to can allow the heart's intelligence to access nonphysical energetics unseen in the visualization.

Heart Awareness Meditation

From the moment of birth to the last breath of life, the heart drums a rhythm to circulate and pulsate the necessities of life throughout the body.

Within that time, its power maintains the life support of the entire body. Every cell is nourished entirely. The brain receives all its needed nutrients and oxygen, and we benefit from the exchange by having the energy to move, think, and feel. Although the heart's significance in its physical role is undeniable, after the unique experiences I've had within my meditations and discoveries about my future self, I began asking, "Is that all the heart can do?"

Accessing the heart's intelligence can come about in many ways. There are two common methods of experiencing the heart's intelligence. The first is a spontaneous burst through the intuition that guides the feeling to act in specific situations, and the second is through a deliberate manner to develop a greater sensitivity to the nature of the heart's intelligence. I often call the developing familiarity with this nature the "language of the heart". Everyone has learned the language of the heart. It is non-verbal and unspoken. It is the very first language we learn. In fact, we spend the first nine months of our development learning the heart's language. How do we learn it? By listening to and feeling our mother's heartbeat, day in and day out. Every second of every minute, for the entirety of our time spent in utero, we are completely rapt by the heart's rhythms. Through our mother's heartbeat, we learn all her emotions, thoughts, and feelings. As we are birthed and grow into speaking and thinking verbally, the language of the heart is lost to the conscious mind; just as a language can be lost when a child is schooled in another country surrounded by other children who speak the new language. Thus, the language of the heart sits within the subconscious. It will be aroused from time to time; however, it can only be accessed more completely when a deliberate action is taken to re-collect its unique vernacular.

Just as there is a process for learning a new language, there is a process for accessing the intelligence of the heart. This can be learned through Heart Awareness Meditation. The ability to tap into the intelligence of the heart is innate. With further guidance and practice, FLP allows for a clear understanding of learning the language of the heart, *and* fluently expressing the heart's intelligence.

The next section is a written description of the guided Heart Awareness Meditation. Similar to the cable meditation, read through the process, and guide yourself through each step. Record it slowly and listen to the playback if that helps you to completely relax into the meditation. Otherwise, you can download the Heart Awareness Meditation on my website at www.zorananda.com.

Sit in a comfortable position. This can be on the floor with cushions or in a chair. Laying down may lead to sleep, so I recommend a vertical spine for a more present experience. Close your eyes and breathe deeply. Soothe your nerves with each exhale. The breath can be slightly audible to help with a feeling of ease as the gentle vibration of the breath calms the body. Bring your attention and focus on the level of your eyes. You may notice that you can "see" the backs of your closed eyelids. Feel how your gaze is naturally settled at this level. Feel that with each exhale, your eyelids, though closed, become gradually heavier. Now, I would like you to realize that there is a second pair of eyelids—an internal pair of eyelids—and as your external eyelids become heavier, your internal eyelids begin to close. As the second eyelids close, you find yourself settling deeper within yourself. With both the outer and inner eyelids closed, feel a deep sense of stillness within yourself. Continue to gaze from the level of your eyes. Now, with your next exhale, being to lower your internal gaze down to your nose. Feel the coolness of the breath as you inhale through your nostrils, and feel the warmth of your breath as you exhale through your nostrils. Remain here breathing calmly, gazing forward from the level of your nose. Now, with your next exhale, begin to lower your gaze down to your mouth. Feel your gaze slowly lower to the level of your mouth. Feel the softness of your lips, the moisture in your mouth, and the hardness of your teeth. Remain here breathing calmly, gazing forward from the level of your mouth. Now, with your next exhale, begin to lower your gaze down to your throat. Feel your gaze slowly lower to the level of your throat. Feel the air move gently through the windpipe, feel the muscles in the neck. Remain here breathing calmly, gazing forward from the level of your throat. Now, with your next exhale, begin to lower your gaze down to your heart. Allow the journey to the heart to be smooth and gentle. Allow as many breaths as needed to guide the gaze down easily to the center of the heart. When you have arrived at your heart, inhale and feel the lungs expand and hug the heart, and on the exhale, feel the lungs empty and give space and openness for the heart to soften. Remain here breathing calmly, gazing forward from the soft and welcoming space of the heart.

Spend as much time here as you like. Continue breathing steadily with an easy rhythm of equally paced inhales and exhales. Remain here until you are ready to return. Now, with your next inhale, raise your gaze up toward the throat. Remain here breathing calmly. Now, with your next inhale, raise your gaze up toward your mouth. Remain here breathing calmly. Now, with your next inhale, raise your gaze up toward your nose. Remain here breathing calmly. Finally, with your next inhale, raise your gaze up toward your eyes. Remain here breathing calmly. With your gaze settled at the eyes, slowly begin to open your inner eyelids. Focus your inner gaze on the backs of your closed outer eyelids and notice how you have returned once again to the natural settling place of your awareness. With the inner eyelids open, feel the heaviness of the outer eyelids rise away as you blink your eyes open.

Reading the above meditation may be tedious; however, the process is necessary. The body needs the time to enter and exit smoothly for harmonious programming to take place. Consider it like this: when entering and exiting a dream, typically, there is a process. A transition occurs of blending from deep REM sleep to waking. In the atypical circumstance of a nightmare or disturbing dream, the process can be cut short right into waking. What happens? The body is in a kind of shock; there is disorientation, exhaustion, and discomfort. Guided meditations are likened to entering a kind of dream state. Thus, it is important to avoid disorientation or shock by allowing the transition process to be smooth.

When I began offering this guided meditation in the monthly series of FLP meditation, the participants noticed a great difference in lucidity and vividness. The effect of including Heart Awareness Meditation led to more clarity in daily life decision making. There is a residual resonance that lingers after Heart Awareness Meditation. Though the brain hemisphere dynamic returns to conscious left and subconscious right, the imbalance of left brain dominance is lessened while the connection to the lucid and vivid intuitive stream of information from the right brain is emboldened. Thus, there is a harmony that allows for the left brain to work cooperatively with the right brain's intuition via the intelligence of the heart.

The next step is to combine Heart Awareness Meditation with the cable meditation. Enter the Heart Awareness Meditation from the method written from the previous page. When you arrive in the heart, allow for a troubling scenario to arise, and follow the steps of the cable meditation. Was greater lucidity more available? Was the process of moving along the cable more vivid and lifelike? It was more vivid or not? If it wasn't more vivid, then more time spent moving toward the heart is necessary. The gaze must be grounded at the level of the heart. By grounded, I mean looking directly from the center of the chest, as if your inner eyes have moved down into the center of the heart. Natural after-effects include a sense of positivity, relief, relaxation, and peaceful contentment. These effects are based on the combination of the new relationship with the heart's intelligence and the clearing of emotional attachments to past events, which will be very important to the actual process of meeting your future self. The developed result of Heart Awareness Meditation and the cable meditation is an increased sensitivity to and usage of the language of the heart. Solutions to challenges in daily life are much more easily acquired because there is an assistance that was seemingly missing before the inclusion of the heart's intelligence.

Language develops through repetition. The daily routine of entering the heart will create a bridge between the conscious and subconscious minds. As the language of the heart becomes a fluent expression, the right brain's intuitive manner can flow into the left brain's modality of reasoning. The bridge between the conscious and subconscious is now a two-way stream as the heart has constructed and integrated seamless transference. The constructed bridge and integrated transference are a concluded result to allow the repetition of traversing the bridge to establish a trusting relationship with the language, intelligence, and intuition of the heart. Chapter 2 will look more closely at repetition, its importance, and exercises to further stabilize and strengthen the heart's bridge of integration.

CHAPTER 2

Repetition

The dream is gone. The eyes haven't opened yet. Small sounds from the outside world creep in, along with a quiet stream of thought. The stream slowly turns into a river with rapids sounding louder and louder. With those thoughts comes the realization: "I'm awake."

Upon waking to a new day, there is thinking. Examine your thoughts when you wake up. Can you find patterns? Over the course of a week, you would be surprised how repetitive your thought processes are upon waking. These processes help form the quality of the day to come. As the day begins, thinking turns to speaking to express the inner thought processes and feelings. Because thinking is repetitive, speaking flows out to the world with a list of phrases and reactionary words. The patterning is subtle to observe; a day can go by with phrases repeated multiple times. There is a more in-depth process involved through personal identity that attaches to the repetitive phrases and words. The attachment stems back through childhood where family, friends, and favorite television shows have influenced our internal and external expressions. There is a sense of ownership that develops from childhood into adulthood, and, with little awareness, our actions are then influenced greatly by those adopted patterns. The ownership is necessary. The flow from thought to speech to action drives identity to create and participate with society. Thinking about goals, dreams, and speaking with friends, family, and colleagues lends to making decisions about which jobs to have or careers and passions to work toward, along with many other daily decisions. Examining thoughts, speech, and actions can unveil the percentage of positivity and negativity expressed daily. The examination can also uncover harmful decisions in adulthood. Let's look a little deeper with the three processes of thinking, speaking, and acting.

Thoughts and Thinking

Stop. Enjoy a deep breath. Inhale, fill your lungs completely. Exhale, empty your lungs completely. That in-and-out process is fundamental. It is a natural phenomenon that occurs as a human experience in a multitude of ways. Thoughts and thinking also share an in-and-out process. Normally, the two are considered inclusive. However, with careful observation, thoughts and thinking are quite different. Thoughts are a product of information received by the right brain, then processed by the left brain. Think about that annoying song playing on repeat in your head, or a worrisome vision that vividly animates fear. There isn't a conscious collaboration that occurs to bring about such annoyance or worry; it seems to come out of nowhere and enter the mind.

As the response to the annoyance or worry is nearly simultaneous to the interrupting thought, they are viewed as a package. With closer inspection, the one experience of thought can be dissected apart from thinking by experiencing thought as an inward "pull" and thinking as an outward "push". What kind of thinking occurs during a repeating annoying song or a worrisome vision? Typically, reactive negative thinking: "This song just won't stop! Why won't you just shut up and stop already?" "I really hope that doesn't happen! I'm just so afraid, I don't know what to do." Thoughts and thinking work very well together. We develop the mind for the two to be seamless. Over years of repetition, the relationship between incoming thoughts and outgoing thinking perpetuates patterns of reaction.

With so many external influences from the media, friends, family, and society, the balance between a negative and positive ratio is determined by either a subtle ignorance that develops the ratio seemingly randomly or a deliberate knowing of its effects on life. The subtle ignorance of the negative and positive ratio is a product of childhood, while a deliberate knowing is a product of adulthood. When we are children, the capacity

15

to be conscious of repetitive thought and thinking processes is naturally lesser as we conform to beliefs more easily. There isn't a second-guessing of the potential negativity hidden in the thought and thinking processes, and over time, daily life is shaped and influenced until the ratio is noticeably promoting behaviors that are harmful to the self and others. Adulthood calls for a perceptive maturity to understand the relationship between overt negative thought processes and reactive thinking that supports the negative thought processes. Yet, identity to the thought and thinking processes is secured and habituated, just as unconscious irregular breathing patterns are established and performed without conscious effort. What is the result of having an imbalanced ratio of more negative thought and thinking processes than positive? Throughout the day, incoming thoughts will promote distress and anxiety. Reciprocated and reactive negative thinking seems unavoidable. The call for negative thinking is behaviorally necessary to complete the pattern and cycle. After years of perpetuating the habituated negative thought and thinking patterns, by-products of mental, emotional, and physical health issues manifest. A loop of support maintains the negative thought and thinking processes to perpetuate the manifestation of health issues. Typically, childhood is often the excuse to maintain this loop. Instead of taking responsibility for personal choices that lead to health issues, we may respond with something like, "It's not my fault this is happening, I was raised to think this way. I can't just change myself overnight. It's too late now, there's nothing I can do about it." The responses justify the continued negative thought and thinking processes. The child we hold dear within always remains innocent. However, that child who unwittingly promoted the nature of imbalance is now an unhealthy pattern in the current adult.

Can you recall a memorable childhood experience? Take a moment to recollect a memory where you felt loved, supported, encouraged, and cherished. It might be a memory of a perfect birthday, family vacation, scoring the winning goal in a game, or playing with childhood friends. Looking back on a memory that is latent with positivity remains powerful, even years later. It can inspire happiness from years ago, and the expanse of time is irrelevant when joy arises. The powerful positive memory seems to have no restriction and feels like it occurs in both moments congruently. A potent congruency between the present moment and a past memory is developed by deliberate repetition. Can you recall the brief moments of positivity in your daily life? Can you recollect a conversation last week when a friend complimented you? The congruency of positivity in everyday life is influenced by either deliberate conscious decisions or uncontrolled reactive patterns. The congruency between the present moment and the past recollected memory is much more random through uncontrolled reactive patterns; the potency of recollection is also lesser. Deliberate conscious focus applies feeling to promote a greater potency, thus allowing for congruency to occur easily with more clarity and lucidity of the past memory.

As positive thinking patterns are repeated daily, experiences in life reflect the internal thinking patterns. It is important to realize that developed positive thinking patterns from childhood can be strengthened in adulthood. A reciprocation occurs cyclically as a past childhood memory is recollected. The past memory is brought up, the feelings from the present and past memory are congruent, positive thoughts emerge from the memory, and reciprocal positive thinking patterns support the thought process and feelings. The deliberate use of this reciprocal cycle forces the pattern to arise in the future. Thus, recollected conversations from a day, week, or a month ago are more easily envisioned by a stronger foundation through positive reinforcement. What is occurring is a choice that every moment is meaningful. There is a latent positivity in viewing your daily experiences as meaningful. Simply look at the word itself: *meaning – full*. The experience is full of meaning. The meaning ascribed to an experience is a choice. With a deliberate application of positivity, joy and bliss shine in the forefront of the mind, promoting a potent congruency of feeling positivity in the present moment *and* from the recollected memory.

There is always an opportunity to make healthy changes. Shifting from negative to positive thinking patterns may not be the easiest task; however, this book has many tools within it to help develop the inner strength necessary to become more aware of subtle internal processes. Follow each exercise, chapter by chapter, and each step will naturally promote more clarity, balance, and awareness of your own self-mastery. The future self you are gradually working toward interacting with requires a level of self-mastery that enables a smooth exchange to occur.

Speaking and Expression

Speak from the heart. These four words are very easily put together but are not so easy to perform regularly. Speaking from the heart is a commitment. It is not a slip-of-the-tongue blurb that lacks sensitivity to the quality of language use. Speaking from the heart involves feeling. When you hear, "Think before you speak," that thinking must also include feeling. Allowing time to contemplate the words that are soon to be spoken includes sensitivity to how the words will sound, how the person/people will react, and how the environment will absorb the vibrations. In day to day speaking, there is less awareness of heartfelt emotion. The dominance of logic places importance on reasoning to speak factually and properly without intuition and feeling. However, expression is different. Within expression, there is a natural tendency for feeling and heartfelt emotion. That's not to say expression lacks logic. On the contrary, logic and reasoning are supported by heartfelt emotion. What can occur with the coordination of the seemingly contradictory concepts is more impactful speech and portrayal of the ideas being expressed. The result is an experience greater than simply hearing words. Expression is a cause for stimulation through the entire body. It can respond with a rush of sensation that flushes through the skin to clearly indicate impactful truth, or perhaps causes our eyes to be literally flooded from the power of honest expression. There are various ways to observe how the physical self aligns with true heartfelt emotion and expression. A powerful example is the simple and wholesome guidance from an elder, especially one dear to you. Surely, you have heard words of wisdom that have shaken you to your core, shaken so deep that you awaken the next morning willfully changed and determined to embark on a new path.

Speaking and sharing ideas can be a selfish act, as well. The desire to get an idea across without considering the other person is a cause for their diminishment of contribution to the conversation. There can be an appeal to speaking that is simply to hear one's own voice. If awareness isn't brought to the developed condition of selfish speaking, repetition comes into play by recurring vocal mannerisms that develop into identity and personality. It is embedded into identity to such a degree that any awareness of the other person's feelings is overshadowed by their own sense of pleasure. Imagine a wall is put between two people. The wall is one person's thoughts, thinking, ideas, and vocalization. On a subtler level, the vibration and resonance of their voice adds to the wall to reinforce the barrier on multiple levels. What would it take to break through the wall? It seems almost impenetrable! Have you had the experience of someone talking over or interrupting you? Whether at a friendly gathering or a family dinner, there is seemingly always one person cutting everyone off. No matter how you time yourself, it seems impossible to get a single word in. What effect does repetitive selfish speaking have on the individual behaving this way? First, the ability to listen intently is negated. Even when another is speaking, their own swirling thoughts and ideas are heeded more acutely than the other in the conversation. The listener will inevitably feel that their contribution has little relevance to the dominant speaker. This creates a diminished sense of connection and a strong sense of disinterest. Also, the heart is neglected. It's typically left to function solely as a pump to circulate blood; however, it is most importantly the provider of intuition and feeling. Connecting with the heart can make a conversation spark deeper nuances between people that unveil synchronicities and likenesses that selfish speaking can never achieve. Often many individuals do not learn to incorporate their heart into conversation because, as I mentioned at the beginning of this section, learning to speak from the heart takes commitment.

Stop. Enjoy a deep breath. Inhale, fill your lungs completely. Exhale, empty your lungs completely. Before you continue reading, bring your attention to your heart for one minute. Be still and silent where all that's left is the soft rhythm of its pulse. Do your best to continue to stay there. Continue to concentrate on the pulse. Breathe into the heart. The brain begins to change. A subtle growing pressure builds behind the eyes. Calmness swirls and soothes the body. This is feeling. Speaking from the heart is speaking from *this* feeling. It is significant to reiterate here that speaking affects the environment through vibration. Though the vibrations are unseen, the objects and people around us intercept the vibrations. What was felt before speaking can be felt by others while we speak. When our words are resonant with vibrations of the heart, that feeling of soothing calmness is encoded into the words and what coincides is a change in vocalization and speech. The tone of voice changes, word usage changes, and the amount of speaking decreases because the heart knows how to get to the point. It has two beats, no more and no less—two beats to circulate gallons of blood in an instant.

Commitment. We have committed to speaking a language and have no trouble maintaining that commitment. It drives humanity. Everything we do revolves around speaking, yet speaking from the heart proves to be challenging. It simply is not a primary focus from childhood. There really is no mainstream educational teaching that focuses on the science and morality of speaking from the heart. We receive bits of teachings from parents, friends, and mentors who offer wisdom, but a foundation for continual heart-centered expression has yet to be established. Many teachings around the world offer excellent discourses and practices, and the average human learns that the heart only operates through physiological functions. Fortunately, there are increasingly more scientists and other professionals who are curious to explore the extent of the heart's qualities. There has been recent research regarding specific fascia and connective tissue that surrounds the heart. Past surgical methods disregarded the purposes and significance of this fascia, and it would be procedurally cut away to reach the heart. However, with new developments in technology, the fascia has been observed, and its significance has come to light. Research has been performed on a layer of superficial fascia that embraces all organs and muscles throughout the body to give them form. It has shown that it also acts as a carrier for water. Furthermore, the fascia specifically surrounding the heart is a protective barrier filled with water. More studies have concluded that the heart produces an electromagnetic field. The powerful connection of these discoveries holds a vital revelation that we will explore much more in Chapter 6.

It is not enough to be a verbal creature. Humanity is not simply a hairless animal that repeats the same stories, one liners, and catchphrases. That may sound harsh; however, it's important to consider the animalistic quality of maintaining verbal patterns. There is a mechanism of survival in place. Personality and identity are interconnected with speech patterns, and biases are developed to ensure those patterns are not replaced easily. If a suitable replacement arises, it is viewed in accordance with the personality for a smooth adoption to occur. As long as the identity that has been unconsciously formed by years of patterns and repetition maintains control, replacements occur without heartfelt awareness that biased beliefs cause problems.

A commitment to heartfelt expression is the remedy to the unconscious development of unwanted speech patterns. That may be a bold statement; however, the process is simple. Before speaking out and after thinking about the words, consult the heart. Consulting the heart inspires expression. Each word is felt and weighed while the person/people are considered. A sensitivity to the environment arises to inspire harmony between the expression consulted by the heart and the people receiving the communication. A reprogramming or repatterning begins. The more the heart is consulted with, the more reactive speech is subdued. Over time and repetition, the heart's intelligence will induce a meditative state to initiate an expression aligned and empowered by the heart. The choice to align with the heart becomes second nature, and soon it will be an easy choice to make. The commitment is an enjoyable feeling of interconnection and harmony as the language of the heart is a silent weaving that grows togetherness and bonds of community.

Imagine you are sitting on a bus. It's crowded and loud. There isn't a single person familiar to you. You look around and see everyone in their own world—teenagers playing on cellphones and listening to music, adults reading books or likewise texting on their phones, and babies babbling and occasionally crying. A sudden separation is felt between you and everyone else. There's an awkward feeling of wanting to talk with someone, yet not wanting to disturb them. That separation seems so real. Space divides. The more time spent ruminating about isolation, the expansive canyon widens the divide. However, the gap in the canyon can be bridged.

The next time you're in a vehicle, bus, crowded room, airport, or any place where many people who are seldom interacting with each other, close your eyes and begin the Heart Awareness Meditation. Complete the process of going down into your heart. From there, bring awareness toward two people close to you. For now, two people will suffice. Visualize a bright light within your heart and extend a beam of this light to each person close to you. Extend the beam into their hearts. What is your experience?

Sit with the connection for however long you like. When you feel that gap of separation close and noticeable integration happens, bring the beams of light back into your heart and slowly make your way back up to your eyes from your heart.

This simple exercise can be a powerful method that alleviates disconnection and negative mind chatter about fellow human beings. When you speak from the heart, immediate goodness will result. You may find a new kind of encouragement to speak with people around you as the usual insecurities and concerns about talking with strangers will be significantly lessened. Synchronicities emerge to encourage interaction. You may notice objects with qualities that signify similarities that will allow interaction to be more naturally welcomed. The initial communication of noticing the synchronicity can help draw the other person inadvertently into their heart as well. Though it is much more deliberate and intentional, it seems like a coincidence when a conversation spontaneously arises. The event is marked by a collaborative effort from different sources of inspiration. Perhaps the two of you are wearing the same shoes, or their backpack has a keychain on it that reminds you of a toy you had as a child, or their eyes are the same Shaker iris type as yours. Beyond the physical, information arises that is evasive to the reasoning of the mind but picked up by the heart to encourage interaction based on the unassuming synchronicities. However, the heart informs the mind that synchronicities are beneficial. The feeling of excitement drives the motivation to step out of the separation that everyone easily conforms to, and instead express, "I like your keychain. It reminds me of a toy I had when I was younger."

Simply noticing these synchronicities may be enough to create a sense of connection and acknowledgment that there was a subtle influence from your future selves. The pleasant event is now within the memories of you and the other passenger. A significant aspect of FLP is knowing that your future self is currently looking back through their memory at you right now. Knowing that we all have hearts that are interconnected silently can inspire a joy within that paves the way for viewing the environment with a graceful outlook. Though the bus, airport, or crowded room may still exhibit a tone of disconnection between everyone, within is a noticeable awareness that everyone was brought together to simply be and experience togetherness in that space.

The heart brings about alignment. The thought and thinking processes align with expression. Imagine the astrological sign Aquarius.

The figure of a person pouring water is a symbol of giving, a transference made wholeheartedly. The flow from thought to word is likened to the water flowing from the vase held by the figure. The significance of such flow is awareness of intention. With a well-founded heart connection, the intention to flow its intelligence through the mind and into the expression arises at the forefront of consideration and conscious decision making. However, for the language of the heart to stem easily from thought to word, there are necessary processes that must be applied as often as possible to enable the flow of the heart's intelligence.

Action and Reaction

"I can't believe they said that! Are you going to do something about it?" This is a response you may hear when an "unbelievable" event is explained. Reaction is a natural ability within the tool kit of human expression; however, its use is usually subjected to spontaneous outbursts when deeper introspection and consultation with the heart are needed. The quick, knee jerk response associated with reaction is both a habit and a choice. With or without awareness of consequence, thoughts and thinking are acted upon, and a choice needs to be made. Space exists between the habitual reaction and the choice to act. Though the process may be quick, there is always an opportunity to choose another route.

The vast uniqueness of humanity is overwhelming. Each of us has a complex array of subtle nuances in reaction, yet we can all be generalized into smaller categories, such as positive and negative, love and fear, exciting and mundane. These can lump each one of us into a list of personality traits and characteristics. It is fascinating that even within these generalized groupings, the fear one person experiences, for example, can vary to an extreme degree on the spectrum compared to another person. At the root of all these perceived differences in behavior, we share a basic mechanism to react without conscious thinking. A hardwiring occurs in childhood. Initially, it is a mirroring and survival mechanism that sparks a quick decision and action with necessity. Later, this becomes a conscious or unconscious justification as it is perceived to be in alignment with a conscious or subconscious personal identity. During a reactive moment, there typically isn't a noticeable paralleled reasoning that the reaction is unjustified or could be different. It's only after the reaction that thoughts of doubt, shame, or regret arise. It is possible to question our positive reactions; however, it is with more negative emotions that there is a higher likelihood of ruminating over our habitual reactions. Our self-image and the extent of the relationship we have with the people we are interacting with can also be a factor in rumination. To put the concept of this mechanism into action, imagine an argument you've just recently had. What happened? Do your best to recall as vividly as possible the words and the physical responses to the emotions of what you remember seeing. Can you recall during the argument when you lashed out or expressed anger or frustration if there was any kind of impending simultaneous thought you shouldn't react that way? Or did the thought emerge after the reaction? It is uncomfortable or embarrassing to recall, but it is a significant self-assessment. Why is it important to recollect these memories? Hindsight is always 20/20. The ability of hindsight surfaces when peering into memories, but there is a lack of this amid a heated argument. Though the memory may be triggering and the need to justify or defend the reaction may arise, the emotional surge of a memory compared to the experience is notably less, and we can replay the memory repeatedly with lesser and lesser degrees of reactivity. As the memory is observed, the moment when the reaction can be caught and altered is captured with much more clarity. While experiencing an argument, the emotions overwhelm the ability to take a step back and observe. Thus, the most justified action is reactivity. Consider another situation that isn't an argument, but still warrants a reaction. Perhaps you have signed up for a course that builds confidence and life purpose. You are excited because you know it will be beneficial. However, the thought of being in a room with fifty other strangers working on themselves makes you feel anxious.

With consistent practice, we can become familiar with and aware of our unique reactions. What would happen if, in these moments, we consulted our hearts?

Focus on your heart, breathe, and feel the lungs hug the heart. Close your eyes for a moment and feel the hugging breath. Go back to the example of signing up for a course on confidence. How much anxiety do you feel now? Although you are only reading and imagining this scenario and not experiencing it in real-time, understanding the sense of calm that could come from practicing the Heart Awareness Meditation is still quite powerful. Perhaps you already had a sense that it was the only logical course of action! This may be because it has been a function that has occurred throughout your life. Biologically, our bodies also support this shift in attention by controlling blood flow. In moments of high reactivity, blood is being supplied to areas of the body to support the reaction, such as the nervous system, adrenals, and the endocrine system that ready the body for fight or flight, to any degree. When we stop and consciously focus on the organ that is flooding these areas with blood, changing our attention will change where the blood goes. Deepening our breathing and directing it into the heart will support the heart as it begins to empower other areas of our body, and where that reaction comes from will have less influence. The power of the reaction will deepen, and a new response will arise. The heart is a powerful being. I say *being* because of its great ability to operate an entire body and maintain its life force. The heart's role has a physical *and* spiritual responsibility as. It is a being of multidimensional operations.

Acting from the heart is no easier than speaking from the heart. Acting from the heart is much more than placing attention on basic movements and functions. Focusing on your heart while walking, breathing, listening, and speaking is important; however, there is another aspect to the heart-focused action.

Life purpose is guided more potently when the heart is deliberately involved. Committing to the heart and its guidance will unveil inspiration and insight into greater life decisions. The information that is received from the heart isn't fantasy or daydreaming about what could happen in the future, but a much more powerful inclination. Repetition is a concept we can make work for us. Repetition of Heart Awareness Meditation can also help develop the discipline to discern when the left brain is merely fantasizing. It could be that up until this moment in your life, repetition has unconsciously worked against you and empowered parts of you that are not necessarily in alignment with who you hope to be. How can we learn to discern between these experiences? Perhaps the following scenario is relatable to you. Have you ever tried to meditate only to spend ten minutes following thoughts that take over every second of meditating?

The thought dovetails into a visual scene, and the images repeat over and over until your focus is entirely gripped by their detail and perceived significance. That is fantasy. Soon a flash of stillness brings the reminder, "Oh! I'm supposed to be meditating!" You might have shifted your focus back to your breath and returned to a meditative focus; however, as the fantasy was followed, it was reaffirmed. The mind sets it aside as a memory to draw on subconsciously. The desires latent within the fantasy hide the mechanism of repetition that is embedded within the unconscious mind. In Chapter 1, we explored the subconscious functions and discovered the realm of the right brain. All the images that suddenly flash and linger come from the right brain. The cause of the flash is *desire*. This forgotten feeling and longing emerges from the depths of the unconscious mind through the subconscious to leave a reminder that it was placed there, to begin with. Images fueled by desires are a great distraction from the heart's guidance as they can provide comfort from the suffering we experienced in the past. Often, we are unaware that what we hope for is something we felt to be lacking from earlier life experiences. We may have perhaps dwelled upon these desires for a great portion of our lives, repetitively dreaming that if only we could have or be or experience *something that's missing*, then *that missing thing* would finally fulfill our lives. Why is it then, that the heart can quiet these innate and deeply rooted desires? The intelligence of the heart contains *the desire to end all desires.* The heart fulfills the longing of identity. Throughout this book, we will come to understand that the heart can access information from all lifetimes. Thus, it has within it the power to subdue the longing your inner child has been suffering. The longings can vary from the need for attention, appreciation, and security, to healing, success, and wealth. Over this lifetime, the burst of childhood desires repetitively and without awareness, unwittingly gives life to the desires. Over and over, the bursts will seem real and true, with reaffirming reactive thinking, speaking, and acting to maintain the childhood desires. I want to clarify that attention, appreciation, healing, and success are incredible desires. However, what actuates and manifests their outcomes is heart empowered intention. Dwelling on the desires and fantasizing about their outcomes is an inert function. With awareness, commitment, and discernment, it is time to allow the heart to unveil its realm and prepare its expansive internal space for your future self.

The following exercise is a simple and effective demonstration of how the heart can guide us quickly to the truth. Its continued use is imperative to developing this relationship with the heart, especially in combination with Heart Awareness Meditation. If you can, work with a friend or family member or listen to the recording on the www.zorananda.com website, where all the meditations are found. Have a pen and paper available to record your experiences.

Three questions will be asked in the following order:

1. How are you?
2. What's wrong?
3. Can you do me a favor?

Write these three questions down in your notebook. These questions will be asked one at a time for three rounds. In the first round, each question will be asked and followed with a pause. When you hear each question, allow yourself to answer automatically as a thought. The reactive responses will be what you usually go to when asked these simple questions. What were the responses? When the round is done, write each response down. In the second round, repeat asking the questions in the same order but with a longer pause between each one. This time, after you have an automatic response, pause, and wait for a *second* response. What were the responses this time? At the end of this round, write down the second response for each question. Did you notice a difference? What kind of difference did you notice? Were the secondary responses more positive or negative, or did they create a certain feeling within you? In the third round, rather than going directly for the questions, first, go through Heart Awareness Meditation. When you are centered and grounded in your heart, proceed through the three questions. Note that if you are listening to the recording, the three rounds will happen automatically. The immediate response will arise from the space within your heart. After the questions have finished, guide yourself out of the heart. What were your responses from this third round? Write down the heart response for each question.

Did you notice that the responses were much more uplifting and truthful? This can be attributed to the intuition working in tandem with the language of the heart. Can you recall in Chapter 1 when we learned about the language of the heart? It can only be "heard" through the intuition. Through this exercise, intuition can internally vocalize the heart's intelligence. You can feel it as it is "speaking" through the language of the heart. We can use this exercise to practice becoming familiar with the intuition and strengthening its ability to have a voice through the language of the heart.

The questions listed above are a simple way to elicit and then evaluate a reactionary response so you can explore the heart's intelligence. There is a way to produce your own questions, as well, where you can be guided intuitively by your heart's intelligence to find personal truths. Your questions can be formed from statements. The nature of the statement might not have much depth; however, by changing it into a natural depth of feeling, it produces a gentle yet startling trigger. To make your statements, pick a personal subject that deserves more attention or development. These could be traits of weakness or strengths, interests, ideas, fears, hopes, or dreams. Emotions or attitudes surrounding these statements could range from shameful and judgmental to enthusiastic and curious. Those are normal reactions and are simply signals. Let's look at three examples below.

Statement One: I have an honest, creative/intellectual interest.

First, derive the statement into a question like, "How do I notice avoidance?" Then form a new question to allow for a trigger to occur and form a simple yet difficult response. The difficult response is necessary because it unveils subconscious (possibly suppressed) emotions.

Question One: What am I avoiding?

Statement Two: I am trying to slow down my racing/frantic mind.

First, derive the statement into a question like, "How do I make deeper connections?" Though it doesn't seem like the statement and question relate, they do subtly. The point is to create a window between the conscious and subconscious to invite depth. Do your best not to dwell on the need for a tangible connection between the statement and question to make sense.

Question Two: Why am I lonely?

Statement Three: I am protecting my heart.

First, derive the statement in a question like, "How do I not get sucked in?" The statement can be in the form of a positive affirmation like the one above. Though we may focus on the positive affirmation, underlying insecurity can be pulsating its effect of doubt; bubbling to the surface at "convenient" times to re-enforce its thriving influence behind the scenes.

Question Three: What am I afraid of?

Follow the same protocol of asking each question in three rounds. The level of vulnerability you experience will depend on the statement and corresponding questions. Remember, the main question is to inspire an answer that is to the point. The more you practice this procedure, the questions will become more intimate and naturally more complex. Though there is complexity, there is an obvious simplicity due to the refinement of the total process. The complexity can be the depth of feeling and inner exploration, especially when answering the questions while within the heart.

The whole reason for this exercise is to experience the language, intelligence, and intuition of the heart. With continued practice, everyday situations and circumstances will easily include the heart's intelligence and the newly developed ability to speak clearly the language of the heart. Thoughts, thinking, speaking, and acting will include the heart as it is the consultant of expression. Repeating heart-centered focus will ensure an effortless continuation of living life through and with the heart.

This is precisely what your future self is experiencing daily. Life lived through the heart is their modus operandi. Without repetition, you will inevitably take on an unconscious pattern that strays away from the future self you are inspiring toward, to a future self not at all connected to their heart. Though we haven't directly interfaced with the future self through the complete process of FLP, there are more steps involved that will prepare fully for that moment. The journey has begun, and the adventure is underway.

CHAPTER 3

Merging

I cautioned my student not to step into the light. The portal led to a beckoning realm of complete absolution. "Without knowing your way back, you will never return." I watched him in his stillness and could sense he was contemplating taking the step. Keeping a partial focus on him, I assisted in the guidance of my other students. However, a single moment of neglect, and he was gone. I had taken my eyes away for only a fraction of a second. Acting swiftly, I ran to the portal and jumped in. He was there ahead of me, appearing with the glimmer of a mirage and melting away into the soft and obscuring light. Two looming cliffs were on my right and left with a path in front of me fading into the white. I felt myself merging. I felt myself relaxing and letting go. I snapped into focus and pulled myself back. The students were silent. Another one, gone. Another one, captivated by the eternal.

The above story is from a dream I dreamt many years ago. To this day, it has remained vivid even as a memory. I recall it often and feel again what I had felt within the dream. It had revealed that taking a step into the unknown without preparation can yield consequences, but I hadn't known just what relevance it would have until putting together these guideposts for FLP. How can we possibly prepare for this *unknown*, something we cannot currently perceive or understand? A practice as simple as meditation cannot evolve and advance without preparation. There will be moments that seemingly nothing happens for weeks or months. Sitting down day after day without a new insight, a new depth, or a new feeling can make the plateau seem like the end of the road for meditation. However, the day-in and day-out repetition of sitting patiently will gradually build the capacity. The result of depth and expansion that we search for and yearn for can *only* occur when that capacity has been stabilized. Thus, the desire to jump right into the depth and great eternal expanse needs a foundation of support. Imagine suddenly being on a platform 100 meters up, looking down on an Olympic-sized swimming pool. You've had no experience jumping from that height, haven't trained your body to withstand the water's impact, or prepared any sequence of flips when flying toward the water. Would you do it? The dive into meditative depth requires work and effort to train toward that kind of dive. Simply sitting and closing the eyes isn't enough. Just as there would be a consequence of flipping through the air without any prior experience and smacking hard into the water from 100 meters, there is a consequence of diving into deep meditation without proper preparation. This is also why new students to a meditative practice don't typically experience deep meditative states in the beginning.

A safety mechanism is in place to prevent ourselves from the complete exposure of the divine eternal expansive consciousness. Its placement ensures that we remain attached to the physical experience of life. The experience of being enveloped by the divine consciousness in an isolated incident without preparation can be overwhelming. As we begin the practice of meditation, the expansive consciousness is streamed in a bit at a time to gradually process and become familiar with. The result is *merging*. Over time, with a dedicated practice, our current physical sense of consciousness merges with our greater eternal expansive consciousness: the future self.

So far, we have explored three techniques to allow the heart to unveil its intelligence: Heart Awareness Meditation, Re-cognition, and Repetition. These are the first stages of setting a foundation for a deeper exploration of consciousness. The next voyage of merging is the halfway point toward easily communicating and connecting with a future self. Merging is an act of wholeness. It occurs by the process of connecting into the heart. Once settled and grounded into the heart, the left and right hemispheres of the brain harmonize; rather than operating in their usual dynamic of dominant-submissive hemisphere interaction, both sides are abiding by the control of the heart's intelligence. Merging is a powerful aspect of FLP. With the heart leading the brain's operations, diving into deeper meditation is much more accessible. Compare practicing Heart Awareness Meditation, Re-cognition, and Repetition to preparing to dive from the 100-meter platform into the Olympic-sized pool. The exercise of merging will be the tool needed to rise from the plateau and into a new realm of meditative experience.

At this time, it is important to consider that although these tools so far have been quite structured and segmented to assist in creating understanding, the goal is to have a personal and visceral connection with your heart. With the structured guidance of these meditations and experiences, pay attention to the subtle nuances of the relationship forming, your heart pulling and guiding you into yourself. During meditation, you may begin to feel a sense of peace, or settling, you may feel a natural relaxing as you are pulled into a deeper relationship with the heart, or you may come to know what stepping into an expansive realm feels like, both in and out of the meditations. The half-suggestive visuals and tugging of your thoughts could become replaced with striking clarity of your future self and a complete sense of neutrality in your logical brain. If you don't relate with these descriptions just yet, remain patient and stay diligent in your practice. Like any relationship, as much as the heart is available to you, you must also be available to get to know your heart and your future self. These relationships are alive, and will develop organically as you become familiar with them. With the understanding that the purpose is to pursue these relationships, let's continue onto the next concept within merging.

There is a blending of experience occurring always. Every action leads to more actions. Growth is happening inevitably as movement blends one part of an environment with another. Imagine your house or apartment. As you enter the front door, noticeably, there is an entryway, living room, kitchen, bedroom, and other rooms, given the size. Each room has its own purpose and function. Also, each room has its own life. The paintings, appliances, cabinets, dressers, and other furniture all give life to each room, making each room unique for purpose and functionality. Yet, when we walk from the bedroom through the hallway to the living room, there isn't a pause in movement to suggest that realities have changed or that life in the room has changed. The transition is smooth as we merge one room with another. Similarly, on a larger scale, as we leave the house to enter the reality of the outside world, more transitions occur. Once outside, we enter a vehicle, take a walk, or hop on a bike to get to the store. Again, the transition from the house to the outdoors to the store is smooth and unhindered by the fascination of how each reality is separate yet interconnected. It is easily accepted. An entire life up until this very point has been lived, moving from place to pace and all over the world, seemingly without noticing that each step is a change in reality. This brings us to the next question of transitions: what about the transition between the inner mind and outer world?

Everyone dreams. Dreaming is not limited to the night. It is not solely comprised of the random happenings just before waking up that are either fervently remembered or forgotten instantly. Rather, everyone dreams *and* has ideas of what will happen next in life. Inside the mind are wondrous and inspiring musings that one day great things will happen. And there they stay. Life continues. Movement to and from work continues, movement to and from favorite restaurants continues, and movement to and from bed to sleep continue day in and day out, and the dreams fade into new dreams. The two worlds are kept separate. The smooth transitions experienced in physical life are like the smooth transition of dreams that change. During childhood, those dreams consist of being a singer, professional athlete, doctor, or whale conservationist, and as that child grows, the dreams transition from one to another. However, there is a point when the two meet, where the dream meets the dreamer and becomes a reality. What usually happens, though? That dream has been dulled over many years to meet the expectations of the outside world. Albeit family, friends, media, school, or other looming authority figures, the dream has been diluted to a "reasonable goal" that is either openly mocked or perceived as a naive ambition than what those dreams truly are: a purposeful, greater service.

Awareness within the heart is now more necessary than ever expected. In Chapter 2, bringing awareness into the heart was a practice. Learning deeply about the intelligence of the heart was a step toward learning the language of the heart. Moving beyond our current understanding, we must now use the tools we've forged to discover the intelligence of the heart. Finding its intelligence requires the knowledge to merge the outside world with the inner dream world by funneling the two together through the heart.

In the sections below, there are several quotes from Dr. Catherine Shainberg's book *Kaballah and the Power of Dreaming* to help create a deeper understanding of your future self and FLP. I encourage you to read her book as an additional resource to gather further knowledge of the power of dreaming while on your own journey of self-mastery.

Dreaming

You are dreaming right now. Not only you, but everyone dreams continuously while awake. In her book, *Kaballah and the Power of Dreaming*, Dr. Catherine Shainberg beautifully details the natural process involved with dreaming and how to unlock its power. In Chapter 1, I spoke of the environmental scanning and flash frames the right brain produces perpetually. Dreaming is the result of those functions. When each frame is merged together, a motion picture is streamed to showcase images as movement. Dr. Shainberg describes the process as follows: "Dreaming emanates from our right brain, which, along with the rest of our brain, never stops emitting nerve impulses. This is a natural result of being alive. Like breathing, it goes on day and night" (Shainberg 2005, pg. 1). The continual process of dreaming is mostly unnoticed. With eyes wide open and living through bodily action, dreaming is separated from waking life. Upon falling asleep and entering into thoughtless unconsciousness, a veil is placed between the waking and dreaming states, even though waking life is a dream itself. Dr. Shainberg further explains, "Dream acts on the physical world. The images may be "fantasy", but their effects are real. Imagination affects the physical and vice versa" (Shainberg 2005, pg. 9). My childhood experience is a direct example of such a function. Acting on the intercepted dream vision of the white truck saved my life.

Understanding that the process and effects are natural, we can assume everyone has had these experiences to some degree, even if the intuitive guidance has been disregarded or unnoticed. It is important to consider and realize the necessity to develop a sensitivity and skill of utilizing the flash frame dream visions in daily life.

The relationship between the physical self and the experience of a self in a dreamlike state is tied together by memory. Let's delve into this statement to better understand how dreaming connects us to FLP. We think and know that the world around us is real through direct experience and by the ability and capacity to recall memories of this life. That same process occurs through dreaming. The unconscious blankness slowly forms a visible blackness that gives rise to images and movement. The movement has life—great adventures or mundane situations that have a likeness to "real life" occur. The experience is had, and a memory exists to be recalled. Why, then, are they viewed to be so different? Or why are dreams perceived as insignificant? Having a view that undermines the importance of dreams creates a separation between the two worlds. The body in real life is the body in "dream life". Dr. Shainberg compels us to, "Understand, then, that the true juncture between the two worlds is the body" (Shainberg 2005, pg. 8). The body as a system of physical, mental, emotional, and spiritual being extends and expands from world to world of experience, from daily living to nightly dreaming, perpetually frame by frame every nanosecond. The body is a medium for greater experience of dream awareness during the day and night, and fluidly merging all movement.

Body

"Your sensations are the pathways in *both* directions, to the concrete *and* to the dream world. The senses act as doors that swing in or out at will" (Shainberg 2005, pg.8). Often, we associate dreaming with being entirely "in our minds", and it's not typically expressed that the body is being used to daydream, fantasize, or dream at night. Likewise, looking up to the corner of the room or gazing into the expansive blue sky and conjuring images isn't simply a mental fabrication. Dr. Shainberg expresses in the above quote that the body's senses are streaming into the mind to create the movement of the images. In Chapter 1, we explored the function of the right brain. Its purpose is to create images continuously. When we participate in the right brain's production of images, they come to life. The more sense we stream into the right brain's imagery, the more vivid they become. As Dr. Shainberg states, "The inner world of the right brain is three dimensional" (Shainberg 2005, pg. 9). This explains "zoning out". The right brain's inner world can look so real that the rest of the brain can't tell the difference. This results in time spent in a whole new world of experience away from the more solid physical experience.

Contrary to the belief that the mind and body are separate in dreaming, Dr. Shainberg helps us to understand exactly how the physical self is used in this process. "Your body is the boundary and the link. Being securely grounded in your body, with a strong habit of paying attention to the messages your senses give you, maintains your access to both worlds while, at the same time, safeguarding you from the danger of losing yourself in either" (Shainberg 2005, pg. 9). This important quote touches on what was mentioned at the beginning of this chapter. Preparation is more than necessary; it is a safety requirement. The habit of paying attention also builds trust. The more grounded you can be, the more you can trust yourself to go deeper into the experience and exploration of the inner world of dreaming. The trust of returning safely is also formed. Recall the process of Heart Awareness Meditation. The steps leading into the heart are retraced when coming back. Of course, you can simply open your eyes after going down into the heart; however, the result is noticeable disorientation and ungrounded senses. Depending on the extent of the depth reached, dizziness and confusion can result if suddenly returned to the body. It is important to consider what is more efficacious to form as a habit: the ungrounded and disoriented feeling from a sudden shift to physical awareness, or a gradual return that blends the deeper meditative state with the physical awareness. Forming a habit of a gradual shift holds two-fold benefits. Not only does it help us to better understand through experience how closely connected the world of dreams is with our physical world, but a strength of will and patience is developed as well when practicing the entire Heart Awareness Meditation. An eagerness to return out of the heart can arise that must be met with the strength of will and patience. Conversely, a desire to remain and not return can arise. The strength of will and patience acknowledges that it's time to return because no more depth can be pursued in that session. The time to transition back must be smooth and gentle.

Mind

Dr. Shainberg also examines the role of the mind in dreaming. "We could say that our mind exteriorizes itself. It recognizes itself outside, in the patterns of the created world, and reflects back to itself, inside, those patterns which best reflect its being. This quest for self-similarity progresses to incorporate ever-expanding coils of a spiraling web of understanding" (Shainberg 2005, pg. 24). The transition from a dream to waking life is generally smooth. There is a relative acknowledgment of self that the dream was dreamt by you, and awakening is brought into the real you. Have you ever had a dream that was completely far removed from the world you live in? A dream that was completely foreign to anything you have ever experienced? Yes, most of us can recall a dream in a time or place, unlike our waking life. The sky is a different color, the vehicles are of a different shape or form of technology, the animals are strange varieties, and there are two moons. At the same time, it might not be so foreign when considering that everything contained in a dream is only a reflection of the physical world that we experience every day. Even if there are contortions and wild interpretations, the foundation is still grounded in the resemblance of the physical world. Thus, dreams are prevented from showing a complete alteration of perceptive reality. The above quote by Dr. Shainberg emphasizes that the nature of the mind ensures that its contents are a replication of what is experienced in the external world. Expanding on this understanding, is it possible that a shift could occur to have an experience of consciousness that is *not* grounded in physical reality?

"Perceiving the inner world requires a movement opposite of what we are most used to. Therefore, it is necessary that we work consciously at the task of doing it. When we turn inward, what do we gaze at? Not form and pattern, but an empty space" (Shainberg 2005, pg. 28). The antithesis of physicality, which is difficult to describe in words but simple to recognize once experienced, is ever-present. Physicality is a direct experience of reality through the body's limitations. The inverse of this would be an entirely unknown and unseen existence that has not been and cannot be experienced by the body. In a cosmic oxymoron, it occurs simultaneously with a parallel to the reality of nonphysical existence that is only accessed through conscious methods. More confounding, the transition between a reality full of occupied space and nonphysical existence occurs so rapidly that they can *appear* to exist as one reality. With eyes closed, the empty space of blackness can stretch without borders, but the construction outside, birds chirping, TV chattering can all be heard and blend into our idea of "empty space." As long as there is identification with the physical world, the inner dream world will only be filled with representations. The dream world can become vivid with lucid movement, but the consciousness of a greater awareness cannot become greater than our awareness in the physical world. Regarding accessing the nonphysical existence, the extent of our awareness of the physical world can create a kind of limitation grounding us in our known reality, however dreamlike and foreign it may appear. Simply, one illusion will be replaced by another.

Merging is necessary to allow entry to the empty space of a nonphysical existence through the heart. In this space, a realm can be experienced that opens a portal to the future self. The Heart Awareness Meditation is a precursory foundation for merging. Once the left and right brain hemisphere functions have been reversed, the empty space of the mind can remain without physical world representations. At this time in your work, a decision through the heart can be made to *feel* rather than *think* within the empty space. Many individuals have shared this kind of experience from workshops and meditations I have led, stating that all verbal chatter and visualization had ceased. Perhaps you have not yet reached this space within your heart and have a string of questions: What happens when the future self shows up? Isn't that an illusion? Wouldn't it be the same as a representation of the physical world in the dream world? The simple answer is no. When we imagine a future self without any of the meditations in this book, there is control of movement from the left brain. Reasoning tries to show the future self, based on our current beliefs, biases, and know behaviors, whether conscious or unconscious. We fabricate the future self from what we think of ourselves and how we would like to see ourselves. That sense of control is also present in dreams. The conscious control is in the movement through the dream and any reaction to situations, and the subconscious control is keeping the dream as close to physical world representation as possible. However, to experience the future self, we must be in a state where they can arrive without any bias or sense of control. The result is a future self of any age, and even beyond this life. Many people are surprised at the change of age in each workshop they attend. My experience with Amareld is a clear example.

Spirit

"Spirit has been released, and we are alive, a new being taking its place in the outer world" (Shainberg 2005, pg. 42). Though Dr. Shainberg is speaking about the birth of a newborn, the context of birth in the above quote can be shared with the experience of newness after emerging back into the world after a deep and profound meditation experience, especially after exploring the depth of the heart for the first time. Both conscious and subconscious processes are encoded by the heart's intelligence. Thinking, speaking, and acting align with the heart more easily. However, the exploration must be maintained regularly for the residual resonance of the heart's intelligence to continue as a deliberate influence. Large gaps in time between meditations will return influence to older compartmentalized patterns or allow for new patterns to emerge similar to those older ones.

The body, mind, and spirit are a trinity of influential harmony within the heart's intelligence. These three elements of being can all be expressed and explored through meditation. The practice of traveling downward to the heart (body), experiencing the vast open space of the heart (mind), and filling that space with the wisdom of the heart's intelligence (spirit) is a cause to return to physical life with an open channel to stream that wisdom through clear intuition. Just as there are tools used to enter the heart and become aware of the vastness of its space, there is a tool to call forth its inherent wisdom. That tool is the mantra.

Mantra

The effectiveness of a mantra is mainly due to persistent, continual usage. At first, it will seem like there is no effect other than internally hearing the repetition of words. However, it's important to remember that it's not necessarily the words that are doing anything, but more notably, your own focus and understanding of the mantra's meaning.

Many hundreds, if not thousands of mantras, exist in many different languages, from many different cultures. Because of my personal connection to yoga, the mantra you will learn in this chapter will be in Sanskrit. With that said, there will be an English translation, and whether you choose to chant the mantra in Sanskrit or English is up to you. What's important is not so much which language the mantra is chanted in, but more when and where the mantra is chanted.

In yoga, there are three methods for chanting mantras: out loud and clearly audible, whispered and only audible to yourself, and silent and only known and heard within. Consider each method's level of effectiveness. Though it seems that the louder it is and more noticeable in the world, the stronger it would be, it is actually the opposite. The softer, the quieter, and the more internalized, the more powerful the mantra is. The mantra is a driving force that propels the mind into a focalized point of concentration and focus. Think of your mind as a cave. When the mantra is chanted, the cave is filled with vibration. Imagine that the mantra is forming geometries and visions of cymatic waves all around. What would the cave/mind look like without the mantra and instead a cacophony of random thoughts? There is a significant difference between random thoughts reverberating in the cave and the mantra echoing and harmonizing in the cave. The random thoughts can cause dissonance and internal turbulence. On the other hand, the mantra is a resonant structure of vibration that creates a geometric vibration within the cave that allows for the space to enable concentration and focus. And that is another big difference, the mantra *enables* concentration while intruding thoughts do the opposite. If you were to sit down, close your eyes, and start chanting a mantra right now, chances are it would take quite a while before you felt any significant concentration and focus. That is mainly because chanting mantras may be new to you. If that is not the case, and you have some experience, I implore you to initiate Heart Awareness Meditation and one of the exercises from the previous chapters. You will, indeed, notice a significant difference.

So far, you have learned the necessary tools to inspire healing within your subconscious mind. As you have entered the heart to begin the process and journey of traversing the heart's great expansive realm, the moment to contact your future self is nearing actuality. Here, the mantra is the next step to further a merger that will allow for the heart's nonphysical realm to be experienced first-hand, the very real Spiritual Heart – *Anahata*.

Jaag Anahata Anandoham

Let us take a close look at the etymology of *Jaag Anahata Anandoham*. Its origin is Sanskrit. My intention here is not to go into the history of Sanskrit or to speak to any lengthy extent of the language. This section aims to get an idea of why I had put these three words together; to delve deeper into the expansive realm of the heart.

> *Jaag* translates to "awaken".
> *Anahata* translates to "un-struck sound".
> *Anandoham* translates to "I am bliss".

When we look at the word *Anahata*, it can be broken down into different words:

> *Ana* translates to "breathe".
> *Hata* translates to "struck".
> *Ahata* translates to "un-struck".

When we look at the word *Anandoham*, it can be broken down into different words:

> *So Ham* translates to "I am".
> *Ananda* translates to "bliss".

When *ananda* and *so ham* are combined, the S is dropped. So, rather than *anand-soham,* it is simply *anand-oham.*

The way I translate *Jaag Anahata Anandoham* isn't directly into "Awaken Unstruck Sound I am Bliss." Though it does sound profound and mysterious, there is a simpler way for *Anahata* to be understood.

To create a context for this understanding, we can refer to the heart as the "physical heart", and *Anahata* as the "Spiritual Heart".

The physical heart beats. It's consistent rhythm, though continuous, has a beginning and an end. This is the "struck sound" of life. Beginnings and endings are a common duality in the physical world. A clear example is the cycle of physical birth and death, centered around the heart beating through life and ceasing through death.

Anahata is directly translated to "unstruck sound", which is clearly the opposite experience of a physical heart. *Anahata* has many other descriptions that are more metaphorical: unconditional love, that which is not created, and that which is not multiplied. *Anahata* is more closely understood as the nonphysical representation of consciousness, and can more accurately be known as the Spiritual Heart. The nature of the Spiritual Heart is to bridge its realm of unconditional love with that of the physical heart, the cycle of birth and death. However, we aren't so aware of the Spiritual Heart, not so directly and intimately as we are with our physical life and heart. Because of this seemingly natural disconnect, I have translated *Jaag Anahata Anandoham* to "Awaken Spiritual Heart I Am Bliss."

The intention of this mantra is to command. You, as represented by bliss, are telling the Spiritual Heart to awaken. The mantra's vibrations, repeated, produce the means to resonate with the innate wisdom deep within the physical heart. Therefore "to awaken" is to fill the space within the physical heart with the wisdom of the Spiritual Heart. A new life emerges that is directly connected to the Spiritual Heart. The internal change becomes manifest in the outer world, and it is no secret that the heart is now in control as the primary consultant of decision making.

So far, each chapter has an exercise to promote healing before the journey to meet the future self. The exercise of merging is to simply chant the mantra, *Jaag Anahata Anandoham*, after doing Heart Awareness Meditation. The physical heart and the Spiritual Heart merge based on the resonance and harmony produced between the two through the mantra. The mantra builds a bridge. Once the bridge is built and secured, access from the physical heart to the Spiritual Heart is easy and unabated by physical, psychological, or emotional aspects because of all the healing that has occurred.

Healing is always necessary. It is a life-long process. That doesn't mean, though, that the power of the heart cannot be accessed because healing still needs to be experienced. Having deeper access to the Spiritual Heart will amplify healing. The healing process will be celebrated and sought out more often because meditative tools and the heart's intelligence are available.

We have come to the end of Part One. Heart Awareness Meditation, Recognition, Repetition, and Merging are now within your new meditation tool belt. Use them regularly and happily. Experiment and observe. The heart is our greatest student, teacher, and companion. In Part Two, we will explore Dream Awareness Meditation, Retrieval, Acceleration, and the Futurist Perspective.

PART 2

CHAPTER 4

Retrieval

I t suddenly had risen from my stomach and into my heart. At first, it was met with resistance. I was confused and shocked at the sob that came out. *I can't. Not here.* Whatever wanted to come out over-powered my refusal. Tears began to swell in my eyes. Sudden flashes of images arose as the tears started to flow. The sobs turned into cries. I was bawling. *It's too late now; everyone can hear me.* There was no end to it. The flash images, like lightning, created a rolling thunder of cries, the tears as rain. Over and over, my mind flashed images of my mother. I was younger and younger in each image until I reached my beginning; I was an unborn child in her womb. Though I was still crying, there was a profound inner silence. A soothing rhythm was present. Her heart, I could feel her heart.

It seemed like an eternity until our teacher Vishvaji finally lead us down into savasana. "Make any sound you like," he had invited. While people were toning and making soft sounds, I let out a guttural, primal, deep scream. It silenced the room. As I lay on my back, the urge to roll on my side and curl into a ball preyed on the weakness within me. *No. I will remain here, open: and vulnerable.* I continued to softly cry, feeling the hurt I caused my mother over the many years of her raising me.

I was in the last week of a two hundred-hour yoga teacher training when this experience occurred. We were guided through a kundalini yoga class that worked upwards through each chakra. The experience with my mother unfolded nearly halfway through working on the heart chakra. The rawness of that day is forever etched in my memory. It is so pivotal that the foundation of the Heart Awareness Meditation is built from that experience.

The night before the kundalini class, our teacher spoke to us about his experience traveling the world and meeting people he couldn't understand or communicate with due to language barriers. However, he was always easily understood, no matter where he went because of *the language of the heart*.

When I was back in my mother's womb during that kundalini class, I could hear and feel her heart beating. Her heartbeat was a persistent, ever-present embrace for nine months; that rhythm of her pulse a reflection of a life beyond the womb that I did not yet know or want, all leading to a continuous wonder of life. And before it all, there is the first method of communication, *feeling*—a rich experience of senses allowing my fetal self to grow and take in all the pulsation, circulation, and vibration. After the class, a new urge had arisen from me; a clear desire to re-learn the language of the heart. Though I may not know every language, or have a desire to speak many languages, I trust that the language of the heart will connect me to every person through the process of sharing FLP.

For years, I have been processing the flashes of memories from the kundalini class. Every memory full of anger and hurt has been tenderly retrieved by my heart. All the feelings were taken in, no matter how hurtful, and gently held, however uncomfortable or unbearable to my logical mind. The heart didn't differentiate between "good" or "bad". The past experiences of hurt were viewed as necessary for learning as if my heart knew that one day, I would remember it all and choose to heal all the hurt, and instead experience bliss and joy from that healing. Over the many years of contemplating the experience, I've realized that the intelligence of the heart has capabilities that seem lost to societal understanding and knowing. Within the heart is a great power; by drawing the energies of past experiences and memories, the heart has healing power.

Fragmentation and Segregation

In Chapter 3, merging was explained as a process of blending that occurs both externally and internally. The practice of merging helps us understand this concept: aspects of our reality, though seeming separate and isolated, are all parts of a whole. This "wholeness" is present from one moment to another regardless of how the objects and places of our physical reality appear or feel distinct and independent of each other and ourselves. The idea that the objects and places are *something other* is due to fragmentation that occurs naturally in our life experience. What is *fragmentation*?

Fragmentation is a multi-faceted experience of segregation. It occurs physically, mentally, emotionally, and spiritually. The first experience of fragmentation is through consciousness; the transition from nonphysical to physical life. However, the first fragmentation isn't the exact moment of complete physicality. The second experience of fragmentation from wholeness is birth. From the moment the umbilical cord is cut, we experience our first physical separation, fragmented from the place that gave us everything we need. From that moment forward, there is a compounding fracture that perpetuates fragmentation. The continual splintering compounds a frame by frame network that builds the very compartments that isolate our memories from one another. The brain is perfectly organized to place each memory through life in its storehouse of experiences. Each compartment holds a piece of consciousness that is encoded with a myriad of feelings and memories. From the first fall you had as a child, to the first heartbreak as a teen, to disappointments and failures as an adult, each experience creates shards of consciousness that make up the past. To better understand the process, imagine consciousness as a great crystal. As physical life is lived, each experience creates fractures from that crystal, leaving shards. Although the cracks and spaces between the fractured pieces and the crystal may grow deeper and farther, the broken shards do not disappear. They are energetically tied to the great crystal of consciousness.

Consciousness will fragment to reflect the growth occurring in the physical world. That's strange, isn't it? It does seem odd that something as omnipotent as consciousness would break into fragments with purpose. Perhaps we can analyze it through a different lens. It may seem more correct to say that as we grow and mature, we become more complete and move beyond a reparative state and into an expansive one. Through the exposure to the fragments of self, we can become more whole by actualizing healing and becoming responsible for our inner growth. Yet, through this same lens, as more information is taken in, the brain creates more compartmentalized space for the new information and experiences and potentially more fragments of separation from the whole. The process from infant to adult progresses from a featureless state to a complex storehouse with millions of compartments. The compartments are the fragments of the original *tabula rasa* or "blank slate" consciousness. Each memory from our past experiences is a piece of consciousness, holding a particular quality based on the reaction during the past experience. If that memory has a negative quality associated with it, it can justify beliefs rooted in segregation. An entire life can be influenced by the fragmentation that occurs internally. The negative beliefs will guide and direct thought, speech, and action. It's important to realize that the energy within the compartmentalized fragments have power. Without knowing it, we access this power every day. As segregation is nurtured repetitively and unconsciously, the power will be more negative in nature and give rise to more self-serving decisions and reactions that cause harm over a longer period.

In many cases, such actions and reactions can benefit the person acting in this way at the moment. The cycle continues that affirms and strengthens the patterns of segregation as there are personal benefits. To bring this concept to life, here are a few examples of how fragmentation is expressed in behavior.

Consider yourself for a moment to be the kind of person who uses the power of fragmented consciousness repetitively and negatively. How the power manifests is being a pathological liar. The choice to be honest is always there; however, the choice of honesty is not within the realm of segregation and its past memory power. In the circumstance of a pathological liar, discontinuing lying will be disempowering to their sense of identity. Each new experience is supported by the fragmentations from their past lies. The power within those fragments will educate the liar on how not to "fail", which, for them, may be reminders of past experiences where relationships or opportunities were damaged by honesty. With each success of manipulating a situation through lies comes a rush of pride and the justification to continue lying. Of course, like many of us, those memories are not without doubt, fear, and insecurity. Guilt is very much present; however, it's a part of the reason to continue lying. Honesty will allow the guilt to bring ruin to everything. Thus, the guilt is a hidden prisoner kept captive within the memories to fuel the continual empowerment of segregation and fragmentation.

Another example of patterns of segregation could be rooted in a time where these self-serving decisions were necessary to protect or defend the individual. A child raised in a violent or neglectful home may have developed a behavioral pattern to protect themselves from the emotional pain of their guardians. A typical response could be to disassociate and disengage from their physical experience to cope with the pain, or perhaps they develop nervous habits such as nail-biting, hair pulling, or skin picking as a means of self-soothing and dealing with pain. The behavior developed is a normal response to an abnormal, painful experience. With each pain experience, the fracture in this child's precious conscious crystal grows deeper and becomes unconscious processing. This fragment of self that feels trapped or incapable becomes triggered in future moments of fear or uncertainty, even when they now have the latent physical, mental, and emotional capacity to care for themselves. Consider how this may affect the child when they grow into an adult who experiences a job loss, a breakup, or a car accident; perhaps they intentionally refuse opportunities and instead perceive them to be unnecessary risks or "too good to be true". At these moments, a change in response to take responsibility for their future or ask for help would be more reasonable, but the fragment of disconnection from self has been affirmed over a lifetime, and the person reacting out of this fragmented consciousness cannot access acceptance of their reality. The fragment of avoidance as safety, though once protective, has been imbued with such an intense negative power that the person cannot see how destructive it has become.

A third example of the driving force of fragmentation can be a situation where there is a cycle of toxic romantic relationships. The person entering these relationships may begin to feel frustrated that they are always attracted to partners who are verbally abusive, emotionally dismissive, demanding, manipulative, disrespectful, or possess other toxic traits. At some point in this person's life, a small fracture of worthlessness may have appeared. Over time and with repetition, acting from this fracture, they have stopped trusting their intuitive sense of people's character and stopped paying attention to their boundaries and desires. They may not be aware of the fragmentation in their lives or that they are acting from this place entirely.

Every relationship they enter only affirms the fragment of worthlessness. It becomes ever more the default view of themselves. Perhaps they even begin to believe they don't deserve to feel safe, loved, or valued in a relationship. Regardless of why this fracture in their consciousness first appeared, the person experiencing their relationship this way is unaware that their self-worth is readily available to them and that they have a choice in changing how they are treated.

I would like to be clear that fragmentation isn't an issue of morality; it isn't as black and white as wholeness is good, and fragmentation is bad. We rely heavily on the overly simplified answers that come from the patterns we develop, and the pursuit of a deeper relationship with the heart will often challenge or contradict our current beliefs. We can examine the circumstances of the examples above. The person who has conditioned behavioral patterns that are avoidant of the truth or destructive to their relationships generally behaves this way because they believe it serves or is preserving their life. The subjective acceptance of these behaviors is a "good" thing, although an outside person may regard them as harmful or "bad". This concept can also be expanded greater than the individual to the effects their choices have overall. To illustrate this idea, the pathological liar will have their own reasons for what they perceive to be good or beneficial, and may even believe their actions are necessary for the greater good.

Similarly, an honest person would not even consider their actions as dishonest. An honest person may be a good Samaritan who pays their taxes, votes during elections, and doesn't litter. Is that person immune to dishonest actions? A quality of segregation can be acted upon without full awareness of the consequences. Just as the good Samaritan, we all pay taxes for roads to be maintained, garbage to be swept from the streets, and many more reasons that benefit the lives of those around us. Some of the taxes also fund bigger projects, such as sending citizens to other countries for military training, combat operations, or war. The people in places that are negatively impacted by a military presence surely question how anyone could support this sort of devastation. Voting can also have devastating effects on a nation depending on the unseen lack of integrity of the politicians elected into leadership, although an individual may consider the person their voting for to be a "good" candidate. Even tossing out the trash from our household can lead to hundreds and thousands of tons of waste filling landfills and causing pollution worldwide. A small subjective action considered to be good can lead to big objective consequences that are bad. For these reasons, the line between good and bad is not so clear. The scale of the interconnectedness of life can feel quite hopeless at times. Thus, it is important to consider that it is our personal duty to reconcile the fragmented segregation that continues to occur. We may not be able to directly change the circumstances around the world that cause suffering and disconnection, but we *can* take responsibility within ourselves to uncover the interconnection between our own fragmented shards of consciousness. To create healing among the entirety, we must find healing within ourselves. We will navigate that interconnection in this chapter through the Retrieval exercise and Dream Awareness Meditation.

It must be made clear, every day, that the rise of memories rooted in segregation is to be healed. The normalized view of "bad memories" calls for suppression and abandonment. However, the energy within these memories inspires intelligence. The simple reason for this intelligence is that these memories are *you*. The attention you give to the fragmented memories can determine how the power within can serve you and others in a harmonious way.

The rise of negative patterns may not always be memories or clear visions. The patterned segregation can be a feeling through intuition. That may be challenging to agree with because, typically, we are told to trust our intuition. However, if our choices are geared and operated by segregation and negative beliefs, intuition can be viewed through the lens of negatively fragmented consciousness. However, intuition is not a part of that fragmented consciousness. We use the power within the fragmented consciousness to manipulate the information within intuition to serve ourselves over others. There is always an option. Intuition is there to aid us, but it's up to us to decide through which lens we view the information.

If we behave from a fragmented sense of self, how can it be possible to learn to integrate that fragment into the whole of our conscious experience *when we aren't aware of what we don't know* that is causing the separation? It can be very easy to confuse or frustrate ourselves, but the answer is very subtle and simple. Again, let us look at the examples from earlier. It has always been the liar's desire to speak the truth, it has always been the desire of a person in a toxic relationship to be loved and treated respectfully, and the individual lacking a sense of safety desires the courage to have faith in uncertainty and to feel peaceful. The truest self always desires to express itself without restrictions or limitations. To heal the segregation and create a connection with ourselves, we must learn to use moments of segregation as guides to connection. Intuition and learning the language of the heart will organically lead to this connection. It can be as simple as a moment of withdrawal from the usual routine. An unexpected experience during the day can trigger a memory of their actual desire that is clearer than ever before. They remember feeling safe, significant, worthy, honest, appreciated. This time, if the individual is paying attention, intuition guides them differently. They feel guilt, hope, confusion, or any myriad of emotions, and instead of turning away from the pain, intuition will guide a deeper understanding and appreciation of the unexpected experience. That is the role of these emotions within. It's a small voice, a whisper from the heart, yet the feeling of an invitation is clear. "This time, will you trust me?" Intuition simply shows us a vision of who we could be based on our own utilization of the information within these other emotions. Perhaps the first time we experience this, it goes almost unnoticed. We may feel it, but we don't act on it. With time, repetition, and a deepening relationship with our hearts, these experiences will compound and become clearer and will be a stronger influence on our future behavior because of integration.

Retrieval and Integration

After my experience in the kundalini class during the two hundred-hour yoga teacher training, I was noticeably lighter, joyful, and at peace. My face shone with a smile from ear to ear, and my heart was beaming with gratitude and compassion. When I used to hear similar expressions from other people, it seemed allegorical to me. Spiritually experiencing the heart appeared to only be a metaphor. However, what I had experienced was a literal flow of joy from my heart all around me. That is what I was living as.

A fellow friend from the training came up to me looking astonished, and asked me how I felt.

"Wonderful!" I replied, echoing his astonishment. "Everything is clear and open. I really needed that!"

With a sense of wonder, he mused, "I do, too! I wish I had let myself cry."

It was clear to everyone in the training what kind of healing had taken place. When someone emotes so strongly, it triggers the intuition in others to be more acute. A natural sense of compassion and empathy is strongly enabled, along with a knowing peace that everything will truly be all right afterward. Remember that the right brain is the channel for intuition. Witnessing a strong expressive emotion helps bring attention to the heart, allowing consciousness to be seated more securely in the right brain. The process to shift from left to right brain feeling can occur unbeknownst to the person logically, yet its presence is felt.

Throughout the day, fellow students approached me, asking how I felt and what it was like. They were not curious about my crying; they wanted to know about the immense clearing and upliftment that followed. I was at peace with my mother and with my entire family. There was a sense of beauty and deep respect for the support I have received all my life for what I love to do. Most significantly, *I was at peace with myself.*

Every flash of turmoil, grief, pain, hurt, and disrespect that I had ever shown my mother gathered. Each piece of fragmented consciousness was brought back together within my heart. Though the energy within the memories was seemingly negative, the heart accepted it without bias and reserve. The pieces were returned to their source. With each retrieved piece, the heart was fueled and empowered. It wasn't a physical empowerment; it was an energetic, spiritual empowerment. This method of healing is a way the heart works that supersedes the unconscious physical operations of circulation. A spiritual circulation was occurring; however, that was within *and* without the body. It was of the body *and* not of the body. The noticeable effect was that my sense of self wasn't solely of my body or identity with who I am/was. The flow of energy emanating from my heart was simply identified as joy and happiness. It was a playful sense of self that didn't need any physical identification to ensure existence.

The kundalini class experience is the foundation of Retrieval within FLP. We all possess the ability to retrieve the energy of past experiences and return that energy into the heart for healing and integration. All of us can heal. This is a very powerful realization and sentence. Perhaps upon reading it, the narrative of your fractures may be speaking up in tones of anxiety or discouragement. *I'm too broken. Nothing can heal what I've been through. I'm stuck this way. Maybe for others, but not for me.* It may also offer feelings of repulsion or contradiction. *There isn't anything wrong with me. I don't have a problem. I only wanted to learn about the future self, not about the past.* We all have a heart, and, therefore, we can heal. The heart's intelligence naturally navigates through all the fragmented shards of consciousness for each of us individually. Periodically, the heart will call for a fragment to be integrated and healed. These will be different experiences for each person. It could happen as a eureka moment during work, a quiet involuntary realization that moves some to tears, or a series of repetitive events that lead us to think, *"Why does this keep happening to me?"* The heart works in tandem with intuition and the right brain. No matter how we may receive the call, we must answer the call to allow healing to occur consciously.

Earlier, we read the examples of several people who were stuck in loops of behavior that caused harm to their life, and asked this question: *How can it be possible to learn to integrate that fragment into the whole of our conscious experience when we aren't aware of what we don't know that is causing the separation?* We must be willing to let the intelligence of the heart guide us to the fragments so that we can retrieve them. At the root of Retrieval is the process of integration.

Can you recall a time when you have forgiven someone? Think back to the situation and recall what you felt in your body as you "let go". In the moment of forgiveness, the memory of the experience that held anger, sadness, or any other negative emotion, dissipates. Was there a tangible relaxation? Did the shoulders soften, and the chest open? Was there a sigh of relief or a gentle release of tears? Was there a spontaneous spout of laughter or a sudden desire to share your liberation with someone? Where does the powerful and intense negative energy go once you begin to feel relief, compassion, and joy? Because forgiveness was chosen, the anger and sadness are transmuted and returned to, or *retrieved by,* its original source. The heart is responsible for that transmutation. A moment of openness and vulnerability allows the heart to draw the energy of the emotion into itself. Integration is the act of harmoniously drawing the energy back within. The process itself inspires a shift in attitude, which allows for a new feeling of joy and bliss to arise and leaves a residual essence emanating through the body. This is precisely what had occurred to me during and after the kundalini class. However, it is unnecessary to undergo such an intense emotional release to draw fragments into the heart. Although we can trust the heart's involuntary divine timing to show us fragments to heal, there is a gentler way to navigate fragmented consciousness. With conscious effort and consistent practice, we can create a path by bringing together Heart Awareness Meditation with the Retrieval exercise and Dream Awareness Meditation.

The earlier section on segregation explained that the fragments of consciousness have power within them. When viewed and experienced from a negative lens, the power in the individual fragment was used to fulfill immediate or urgent self-serving desires. Though viewed as a kind of goodness, the result led to be negatively impactful for others or for self over the long-term. Integration involves viewing the energy within the fragmented consciousness in a positive manner. When perceived this way, a quality within the power arises that is quite different from segregation. There is no interconnecting arc that allows the negatively viewed fragmented pieces of consciousness to combine their innate power. The negatively-oriented fragment relies on its own power and concentrates it to increase potency. As we concentrate on the negativity, it becomes more powerful and easier to focus on. The cycle can gain momentum quickly, and we become frantic, exhausted, frustrated, and lonely. We can choose not to operate from the limited resources of our fragmented pieces of self. However, the nature of integration *does* allow for fragmented pieces to share their power together. As the smaller pieces bind back together into greater wholeness, the positive and infinite energy of the whole begins to absorb and increase the potency of each fragment's negative power, and the energy of the fragment and the whole re-unite. This is essentially how the heart can pull the fragments into itself. The heart is the wholeness. The result is a positive and energizing impact for others and yourself.

Stop. Enjoy a deep breath. Inhale, fill your lungs completely. Exhale, empty your lungs completely. Complete a few more rounds of deep breathing. The actions of in-breath and out-breath appear as separate steps. As you continue to breathe, feel an interconnection between the inhale and exhale.

An interconnection ties together segregation and integration, just as there is an interconnection between the inhale and exhale. As long as you are alive, there is always your breath, just as there is always the experience to breathe. You are the medium for the decision to isolate the power within the fragmented consciousness or create a bridge between the fragments and draw the harmonized energy into the source of its creation—the heart. *You are the interconnection.*

The Retrieval Exercise is an active decision to choose integration. While centered in the heart, the innate intelligence and intuition are present to show you the energy of a past memory. As the viewer, it is your responsibility to act on, rather than react to, what the intelligence and intuition show. The next section will go into detail about Retrieval and how to utilize its potential.

Retrieval

Have a journal or another way to record your reflections ready for post-meditation. Listen to the Heart Awareness Meditation, or quietly guide yourself into your heart by following the steps of Heart Awareness Meditation. When settled in the heart, feel the intention to bring up a past memory to heal in that space. Allow it to rise without control of it. Let it be exactly how it is. You are in a safe space within the heart. When the image of the memory arises, your first instinct will be to focus on the emotions and play out the memory through the emotional lens. However, remain neutral and observe. The image will come to life as movement and sound. Allow the image to move all it wants, yet stay within the heart and silently watch. Bring awareness to your breath. Breathe slow, deep, silent breaths. Within intention, breathe the energy of the vision in your heart. It may be slow; however, guide the emotions, feelings, and energies from the vision in your heart. Continue this process as many times as necessary until the vision completely dissipates. When the image is gone, feel the energy within your heart. Feel the energy merge within as the fragment integrates back in your heart's intelligence. You may remain here and call upon more memories, or guide yourself back slowly.

Take time to return to your body and move your fingers and feel or stretch gently before opening your eyes. Read the above paragraph a few times to familiarize yourself with the exercise. Before continuing, guide yourself through the exercise, or listen to the online version on my website (www.zorananda.com). When you return, reflect on the following question. What did you notice? What was the process like? What did you visualize? What did you feel? How was it to observe a discomforting memory without judgment? I recommend writing your responses and reflections down and any other questions you may want to reflect on. Further insights may arise when writing that can clarify tendencies and patterns observed in the heart's intelligence.

Though the exercise seems easy, it can be a lengthy process. Being at ease with the process is a patience that the heart admires and asks of you when you are within its realm of intelligence. Practicing Heart Awareness Meditation and other exercises are important steps before doing Retrieval. In many meditations, I've had newcomers struggle with simply observing the visions because they would get caught up with the story. Suddenly, they would forget where they were because the vision had wholly absorbed them. When we have a solid foundation built within the space of the heart, the ability to remain calm and observe is much easier. Seeing the vision clearly as an experience that simply requires healing helps to draw it back into the heart. It is a story, a narrative, a fabrication. The merit we give it keeps it fragmented and cyclic. As long as it remains isolated, the story perseveres and maintains the conviction that its contents are justifiable and important. Remember that your healing is always of utmost importance.

Three Phases of Emotion

How would you describe emotions? The *Oxford English Dictionary* defines emotion as a natural instinctive state of mind deriving from one's circumstances, mood, or relationship with others. *The Merriam-Webster Dictionary* also states that emotions are typically accompanied by physiological and behavioral changes in the body. Very simply, emotions are instinctive, intuitive, and physiological feelings. When we think of our own understanding of emotions, the most pertinent conclusion we usually come to is the ability to express them. So much significance is placed on the expression of emotions that we perhaps have never considered other ways of personally dealing with them. If you have not considered this before now, it is important to develop an awareness that there are at least two other ways of utilizing their potency, but possibly many more. Outside of expression, we can all naturally *direct* and *expand* emotional energy. Each "phase" has its own realm of experience and purpose. Let's take a deeper look at each one.

Expressive

From conception to about the age of five, we develop our range of emotions and the ability to express what we are feeling. As we mature into adulthood, the reactive response to situations developed in these first few crucial years of life doesn't change much. The trigger for an emotional response can remain quite similar to when we were children; however, the kind of emotion that releases may differ. Instead of crying when we are disappointed, for example, we may have an outburst of anger. Whatever the emotion, the *reactivity* is still there. With the help of friends, family, or professionals, that reactivity can change to allow the emotion to be expressed more healthily and honestly. However, a true change can only occur from personal effort and acknowledgment.

For the first twenty years of my life, I had many people tell me how reactive I was, how sensitive I was, and how easy it was for me to get angry. My friends and family had put much effort into showing me the tendencies I had of being highly emotionally reactive, and where it was causing strain with them. But my personal mannerisms and interactions within myself still included the reactivity. I am grateful that I have had people in my life share their perspective of me; however, there had to be a personal intervention so that I could access the parts of myself where I didn't have others as a mirror to reflect my own behaviors. Your investment is crucial for creating momentum to empower and encourage the continuous synchronicity of changes that promote healthy emotional expression. This does not mean you no longer express negative emotions. Let's look at anger as an example. Once we learn to express without reactivity, the anger is healthier because it doesn't involve blame, accusation, or harm toward another person. Your investment involves acknowledging that the situation has triggered the anger and knowingly directing the anger into the motivation to act in a manner that serves you and others rather than creating destruction or pain.

Directive

Everything we feel as emotion begins internally. Repeated situations cause reactions that develop in our physiological systems like the nervous system and, by extension, our endocrine system. The entire body supports the experience of emotions as a channel for outward expression. As we live and grow, our experience of life and the interpretation of its experiences justify continuing the patterns that support the reactive nature of emotional expression. It's a one-way flow from internal to external.

When we begin to meditate and learn the process of focusing inwards, the reactive nature of emotional expression can be reversed. Over time, it can be observed that there is indeed an internal flow of emotional energy. It is quite different than outward emotional expression. When emotional energy flows outwards, it picks up on biases, beliefs, personality traits, and behaviors to present a package for the outside world to experience. However, it is only bits of totality that the emotional expression is presenting. When emotional energy is *directive*, it doesn't go through the amalgamation of our identity and personal beliefs. Instead, the energy is channeled and concentrated. Heart Awareness Meditation is the principle process in directing emotional energy into the heart.

The capacity to direct emotional energy into the heart grows larger every time the Heart Awareness Meditation is used because we grow more familiar with the truth of our being. As we are learning, how can we understand and comprehend the difference between expressive and directive? First, emotional expression involves a relationship between the outside world, other people, and self. It doesn't solely necessitate speaking as a method; it can be expressed through art, music, or any other kind of work or creation, as long as there is the feeling that the emotional energy is flowing outwards. By contrast, emotional direction is a deliberate action of channeling the available emotional energy inward into the heart. It doesn't involve the outside world, but it is a relationship between the self and the heart. It is an independent process of interconnecting emotional energy with the intelligence of the heart. I must emphasize that the directive phase of emotional energy unveils a new scope of feeling that you have perhaps not experienced. When directing emotional energy inwards, a different part of the nervous system is now involved with concentrating the emotional energy. Because the body is detaching itself from the external world, a *sense withdrawal* occurs to desensitize the peripheral nervous system. This simply means there is no feeling in the body's limbs, that they don't go numb, or get tingles or prickles like we usually experience when losing feeling in the body. The usual focus we have of the physical body simply shifts into a greater awareness channeled through the central nervous system, heart, and brain. With the peripheral nervous system subdued through Heart Awareness Meditation, the emotional energy can more easily be directed into the heart and concentrated. The feeling that occurs is a sense of becoming small. It's as if you are shrinking and losing all sense of the physical body yet are fully aware it is still there. But what does that mean? What's the point of directing emotional energy into the heart?

Expansive

There is a point when an implosion occurs, and it's not a controlled experience. While directing emotional energy into the heart and having the feeling of becoming increasingly smaller, there is suddenly a simultaneous sense of becoming increasingly larger; you feel like you have grown ten times larger! During the phase of directing and becoming smaller, everything in the surrounding awareness is dark and visionless, and the concentration intensifies. Then, you can see the room you are in, you can see the street and house, and any movement and sounds that are occurring outside, *yet with your eyes closed*. This is an expansive level of emotional energy. Involuntarily and organically, emotional energy has been transformed within the heart. Both expansion and internal direction are happening simultaneously. You feel like you are getting bigger and smaller, traveling outwards and inwards, seeing the entire outside world and a void darkness until there is no distinction between opposites at all. There is simply expansion in all directions. The visions disappear, and an objectless joy arises within a stream of colors and light and circulates through the total expansion. Essentially, this is what we are striving for in meditation.

These processes are an invitation to experience how unrestricted we can be. Expansion gives us a sense of the limitless capacity of experience where there are no boundaries and doubts. There is no end to the expansive phase. It can continue eternally; however, the experience seems to end because of personal capacity. After an indefinite period, the expansion will cease, and consciousness will return to the physical body. Returning to the body will feel like awakening from a lucid dream. There will be a residual feeling that lingers. I suggest waiting until after physical awareness of the body is attained before opening the eyes to allow the feeling to nourish you. Consider this feeling like a seed. Stay with it. Nurture the seed with soft attention of care, joy, and wonder, both immediately after the meditation and as you move forward with your day. That seed will grow into a capacity of longer durations of expansion during meditation and more potent residual effects after meditation.

When we consider the significance placed on expressing emotion through words or other creative ways, the phases of experiencing emotion through direction and expansion seem to have very little to do with emotions as we know them! When we experience directive emotions, it isn't about directing or controlling our expressive emotions. When we experience expansive emotions, we aren't expanding our expressive emotions. This process isn't about taking an emotion we express, like anger, and directing it into the heart to "expand" it into an emotion we would rather feel. This process doesn't use expressive emotion as a guide. Returning to our basic definition, emotions are instinctive, intuitive, and physiological feelings. Words to describe certain emotional experiences such as anger, grief, or delight become unnecessary as we move into the intelligent space of the heart. From the heart space, the experience is not about discerning the kind of energy we are feeling and what to do with it. That is a cognitive and logical question of self-reflection. Rather, it is about how we are experiencing the energy available through practice and learning to recognize and be guided by our intuition into an expansive state of awareness.

The three phases of emotion are a compass for developing a new line of communication and connection with the future self. So far, this book has led us to a precipice to come face to face with an unknown that is anticipated day after day. We yearn for our future self, whether we can consciously identify it or not. Every day we look forward to a better life, a better self that is more successful and at peace with a life of abundance. When expressive emotion is acknowledged within the heart to inpsire healing, directive emotion can implode into expansive emotion where the gateway to the future self opens. To vividly encapsulate a space within the heart and its expansive emotional energy, there is a meditation we can explore to invite the future self to present itself.

Dream Awareness Meditation

The following meditation is called "dream awareness" because of a simple implication: the two work together. When the images and visions occur during the guided meditation, both the dream-like scenarios and awareness noticeably support each other. The deeper you are taken into the guided meditation, the more vivid it becomes. The more lucid your experience becomes, the more aware you become of how real the experience is. The sense of realness to the guided meditation is important and is challenging to experience without practice. For instance, right now, close your eyes and think about your future self. Try your best to vividly imagine yourself in ten years. How convinced are you that your experience of thinking of your future self was real? Most likely, not very convinced. There may have been a visual, but without the emotional connection or vivid life-like interaction. Thus, it is necessary to be placed in a state and space where the interaction is undoubtedly as real as your daily life. For the heart to successfully "take over" and produce the space experienced during Heart Awareness Meditation, the entire process leading up to the meeting of the future self must have all the elements we have learned so far in sequence. The reward of exploring these exercises is a more peaceful and relaxed present life. By consistently meditating, we can develop a closer and more vibrant relationship with the harmonious future self. As you incorporate this new information into your daily practice and find what works for you, always begin with Heart Awareness Meditation, followed by a Recognition, Merging, or Retrieval exercise. It is not necessary to do all these exercises in one sitting. One or a combination can be done depending on how you feel or where your heart leads you. Often, as you reflect on your experiences, you may find that one or a few of these exercises will organically partner themselves during the meditation. You may even create your own exercise. Once you have moved through the process, you will find you are ready to guide yourself into Dream Awareness Meditation.

Dream Awareness Meditation is a guided meditation into the depths of the heart. Because of Heart Awareness Meditation and the exercises, delving deeper into the heart is a much smoother process. In my years of offering meditation, I've heard many people say that entering the heart and exposing its contents is intense and sometimes scary. Why do some people experience fear in a neutral and compassionate space? The answer is simple. The brain can't handle it. More specifically, the personality and identity protected by beliefs and biases see the vulnerability within the heart as a kind of threat to the patterns and habits that have developed, nurtured, and supported you throughout life. The heart exposes the truth of existence. The space and vulnerability created through Heart Awareness Meditation are empowering and integrative. This means that while in meditation, beliefs and biases are in a different realm of experience; they are beyond the scope of comprehension. If not fully in the heart, the brain and its conditioning are still vying for your beliefs and biases. It does not like the unknown, whereas vulnerability is innately encouraged by the heart's intelligence. To allow ourselves to be bolstered by that encouragement, we must consciously choose to trust the heart's intelligence, clearing the beliefs and biases that would prevent further exploration and experience directive and expansive emotional energies. With the open space initiated by the Heart Awareness Meditation and exercises, it's time to explore that space deeper via Dream Awareness Meditation.

Either listen to or guide yourself through Heart Awareness Meditation. Pick an exercise you'd like to do. After you have finished the exercise, guide yourself back, and gradually open your eyes. Take some time to journal and contemplate your experience of the meditation and exercise. Take a little break. Allow yourself to integrate the experience. Listen to or guide yourself through Heart Awareness Meditation again. When you have entered the heart, now begin Dream Awareness Meditation.

Find a comfortable seat, read through the text below and familiarize yourself with the Dream Awareness Meditation to guide yourself through it, or download the meditation on my website www.zorananda.com. The space of the heart has expanded. You feel small within the vast space of the heart. Yet, you simultaneously feel yourself to be large enough to fill the entire space. You realize that you are standing. The space around you is dark yet comfortable and safe. Begin to feel your feet on the ground. Send your attention up to your legs, into your hips, torso, arms, and head. Now, look at your body. What do your feet look like? What do your legs look like? What do your arms look like? What does your body look like? What kind of footwear are you wearing? What kind of clothes are you wearing? Allow these features to be natural. You realize that you are standing on a circular stone. You get a feeling that the stone is floating, and underneath the stone is a bottomless pit. Remain calm.

Far ahead of you is a faint outline of a door. All you see is the dim light coming through the cracks of the doorframe. You are being called toward the door. When you take a step forward, a stone appears under your foot. Take another step. With each step, a stone appears instantly. No matter how fast you go, a stone appears under your foot. You are getting closer and closer to the door ahead of you. Continue forward, step by step. You reach the door; however, there is a stone missing between you and the door, and when you take a step, the stone doesn't appear. Realize that you do not need the stone. When you look back, you notice there are no stones behind you, and there is no stone under you. Take the step forward. As you take the step forward, the door begins to open as a white light floods the threshold of the door. You step easily into the light. You are completely surrounded by light. There are all kinds of colors swirling around you. You notice a floating crystal orb ahead of you. When you approach the orb, images are playing within it. What do you see within the orb? The orb moves toward you on its own and places itself at the center of your chest. You receive a message intuitively from the orb. All the information with the orb is also contained within you. You are the orb. The orb presses against your chest and is absorbed by your heart. A deep sense of joy and peace arises—a joy that is not attached to anything. It is simply joy. The floor in the room appears in front of you as it is time to return. The door opens, and you step into the comforting and safe darkness. Slowly return to your physical heart and back to your body. With each breath, guide yourself back to your eyes, step by step. Notice the sounds of the room around you. Feel a sense of your fingers and toes. Pay attention to your body moving with each breath. Slowly, open your eyes, and sit silently.

Take some time to recall your experience and journal, as accurately as you can, everything you experienced. We have yet to call upon the future self. Dream Awareness Meditation is an invitation. There is still one more step to understand and consider before obtaining the Futurist Perspective. We will explore this in the next chapter.

CHAPTER 5

Acceleration

The room had vanished, and everything went black. Who am I? I felt my awareness shift to the left as I asked the question. To my bewilderment, there stood a being who looked like me! He was wearing white robes and illuminating white light. He had long, wavy hair cascading over his shoulders and a beard to match in length. Recognizing the face, I immediately realized that it was myself I was seeing! I felt such astonishment witnessing myself as this illuminated person all the while being totally outside and removed from him. My awareness shifted again, with a smooth transition and grace I moved towards my illuminated self. No longer observing, but now experiencing, the surprise was washed over in a wave of serene clarity, focus, and presence that was more than noticeable. I was my illuminated self. I looked around the deep blackness all around me when a single cascading light shone down and A small child appeared in front of me, sitting, playing with a piece of chalk. There was hardly any life in his eyes. The boy wasn't drawing anything specific; he was simply making squiggly lines here and there on the ground. "What are you doing?" I asked the boy. He looked up at me with a blank face, shrugged, and lowered his head back toward the ground. He continued his disengaged scribbles.

Trying to help him understand, I explained, "What do you mean you don't know? You have infinite possibilities." The boy was unresponsive. "Give that to me," I stated simply as I took the chalk away from him and instructed, "Watch this." I drew a circle on a black space to the right, slowly and with a full rotation of my arm. The circle became thicker, and as I drew it faster and faster, the chalk dust rose into the air. Suddenly, the center of the circle opened into a portal as I ceased drawing. I gave one last look at the child, and stepped into the portal.

The black room had been consumed by a bright white light as I shot forward into the portal. The sense of growing momentum struck me as a brilliant array of glowing jewel-toned colors streaked behind me. My gaze was focused in front of me. There was a blazing white wave like shape that resembled an S. It was moving in gentle arcs from side to side, up and down, and in all directions. The shape and portal were completely new to me, but without words or thoughts, I could still feel it was imperative to keep my gaze on it. I was being guided and brought somewhere, certain to become lost if I faltered. There was no comprehension of time passing. I was moving forward, yet fixed in concentration and awareness. Suddenly, the white wave ahead turned on its side and stretched out to the left and right, becoming a bright, vast horizon. From the center of the horizontal line, a small emerald square appeared and became larger. It seemed to be a far distance away, and as it came close, I began to see it ripple and shift abstractly, reflecting effervescent colors. Halting abruptly before me, the immense screen hovered and shifted into a holographic image. I saw myself sitting on a couch in my apartment across from a friend of mine, playing guitar together. I watched as the image came to life and became dense.

I began to feel the realness of the image before me. Although I was looking at myself holding the guitar, I could simultaneously feel the instrument in my hands. Not only did I merge with the image, I became completely physical again and was fully in the scene. I stopped playing guitar and sat silently. Looking around the room, I was astonished at how real I had become. Playing a few notes on the guitar, I felt the subtle vibrations. My friend looked at me, bewildered, and asked, "What is the matter?" I realized then with a flash of visions where I had been just before entering my apartment, recalling the black room, my illuminated self, the portal, and traveling forward as bright colors streaked past me like headlights on a highway. Incredulous and excited, I tried explaining it all to him, but it was futile to speak. Everything came out in a mumble of words.

I suddenly found myself returning to the translucent space. The image of my apartment, myself, and my friend lost its lucidity and was receding back in the emerald green square and from where it originally came. The line on the horizon snapped back into the S shape. Guiding me once again, I began to move forward. After traveling for a time, my guide stopped and became horizontal again, but unlike the previous experience, the horizontal line opened into a vast space of rolling hills of energy. The experience was completely serene, peaceful, ecstatic, and blissful—a very uncommon experience in waking life. Yet, it was all normal. Being there was normal and natural. There were no thoughts or words, no sense of individual self. I didn't refer to myself in any way to the person I was before the black room, or while on the journey. However, what was very noticeable was a deep sense of awareness and an overwhelming knowing of exactly where I was and what I was doing. The doing was simply being a complete presence.

I'm going to be honest. My experience at the beginning of this chapter was induced by what Terrence McKenna would describe as a 'hero dose' of magical mushrooms or psilocybin. Regardless of that fact please continue on. The experience is an important part of the foundation of Future Life Proression as it deeply relates to more experiences and theories you'll read about in the final chapters. Therefore, Trying to explain this part of FLP is not easy. It's a personal experience. I know what I've gone through; however, it's not something that everyone will agree with or experience similarly. A nonphysical reality is inconceivable. We cannot comprehend it through theory or explanation. It must simply be experienced. The experience we have as our natural, physical self is a hint to what can be experienced as its antithesis. However, any direct searching for the complete antithesis is a cyclic loop of illusion. It is an exercise in futility while in the non-meditative waking state of left-brain consciousness. The process of FLP is a potentiated shift of perspective to allow for the nonphysical realm of existence to be a forefront realization through the heart's intelligence and clear, intuitive communication via the right brain.

So far, we have explored the heart to such a depth that a doorway has opened to a realm where the meeting of a future self is realized. Before taking that final step to face the future self, we must undergo the method of travel within the illuminated space, similar to what was mentioned in the story above. Your experience will not be identical to mine. There is no right or wrong way to navigate a space and time where our existence is a complete inverse to what we normally experience in waking life. The transition may not visually look like mine, but must involve the same development of comfort and concentration. The acceleration that occurs is a rapid shifting. Though smooth, it can be demanding.

What is acceleration? Using my experience, I will create parallels to the feelings you may have that will help you know you are in an accelerated state. When I was focusing on the guiding S shape, I wasn't moving forward at a constant speed. I felt myself literally moving faster and faster forward. That constant acceleration is necessary; it is a sense of being drawn forward without conscious effort. In the space I was in, and the visuals in my meditation, the shifts between the S and the horizontal line became a smooth process. The acceleration is at such a high rate that it produces the experience of reality within consciousness and awareness, like what I had seen and felt within the holographic screen. What I experienced, I logically had no control over; this is all done by the heart's intelligence and intuition. Yet, there was a sense of control, and this is a paradox that can be difficult to comprehend. Within the accelerated realm, you are allowing yourself to be led by the heart's intelligence, and what you are in control of is the allowing. By allowing yourself to be controlled, you are in control.

When I was having the experience of the S shape turning into the horizontal line and producing the holographic screen, the acceleration didn't suddenly stop. There was, however, a change of perception. The realm around me was contained in an accelerated state. It worked in pair with my focus. As I continued focusing forward, there was a collaborative effort to shift the S shape in the horizontal line and begin a transformative process to continue shifting into a holographic image. I didn't place any ownership on producing the holographic screen, though. It seemed to happen on its own. Awareness wasn't limited to me as the observer and experiencer; it was also outside of myself as the applicator and environment. This extended awareness is difficult to explain and often difficult to create a space within ourselves to understand by experience, but is significant. The entire act of acceleration is a cooperative effort. As I have the sense to continue forward to experience the realm I am in, the realm itself has the sense to participate and experience my involvement. This pairing is what creates the acceleration process. If I or the environment are the sole providers of effort, there cannot be a compounding expansion created to perpetuate an acceleration. In a simple example, imagine you are in a vehicle driving at a constant speed. To maintain a stable speed, you must keep your foot in a steady position. The vehicle also doesn't need to output any more energy or fuel to maintain the constant speed. Once you decide to step on the pedal, this initiates a sequence where the throttle opens, fuel input increases, and the vehicle immediately responds by increasing its power output. The result is acceleration. You and the vehicle are performing together for acceleration to occur.

Consider that during daily life, you're operating at a constant speed. This constant speed is relative to mundane living. There isn't much change. The same routines take place every day. What could it take to turn everyday living into exciting living? Acceleration.

Acceleration is a spiritual process. There is a deeper sense of yourself that is explored, which can experience realms of existence that are inaccessible to the left brain conscious mind. Thus, for acceleration to occur in your daily life, there must be an application of meditation for consciousness to undergo an acceleration into a more expanded awareness and life experience. Each step in this book produces more and more preparation for an acceleration into an expansive relationship with what we are as conscious awareness.

How you go about contacting your future self is a personal and intimate exploration. It's important to allow the question to arise, "Where is my future self?" and act from that moment in following newly provided synchronicities. There is not a logical answer to the whereabouts of the future self. You must learn to feel the answer arise through the intuitive senses. This chapter aims to get a sense of where the future self is with respect to your reality and theirs and the space between. The important part is the space between. How do we get to the space between the current reality and the future self's reality?

Heart Awareness Meditation, Healing Exercise, and Dream Awareness Meditation are the means to enter the space between your current reality and the future self's reality. It's the same space I entered when I experienced the acceleration following the visualization of the guiding S. It's the same space I entered when I met Amareld for the first time. As the space is entered, the acceleration process will initiate through further guidance. The experience of acceleration within the heart isn't going to be the same every time. When I had my experience with Amareld, it was quick. I went from blackness to the great hall she resided in within a fraction of a second. The more you take the time to enter the heart and explore its space, the quicker you'll meet your future self. In the beginning, there is a necessary procedure for traveling to get used to the acceleration. As you become more accustomed to the procedure of acceleration and traveling in this space, arriving to meet the future self will be a spontaneous event. In many meditations over the years, I've had students tell me they had gone far ahead of my guidance. Their ability to close the space between their reality, and their future self increased over the monthly meditations. On the other hand, I have had beginner students have a challenging time keeping up. It's necessary to know personally where you are in the process and not be discouraged if it's challenging in the beginning. This book is an amazing tool to help with that process. The guided meditations and exercises are specially crafted to suit any level. So please, take your time and enjoy each step.

Let us take that final step and meet the future self. Read through the steps below to get a sense of how to prepare yourself and what to expect. Have a writing tool and journal available to record reflections and insights.

Listen to the Heart Awareness Meditation or guide yourself down into your heart. Once you've entered the heart, take some time to be there, and feel the expansiveness of the space around you. When you're ready, pick an exercise that you'd like to do to shift your conscious awareness from your left brain to your right brain. Allow the exercise to take as much time as necessary to feel an integration occur. When the exercise is complete, feel yourself become smaller and smaller as the space around you becomes bigger and bigger. Allow the expansion to surround you. Come back slowly and return to your body. Retrace the steps from the heart back up to your eyes. When you open your eyes, take a brief break to write and integrate the experience into your conscious awareness.

Listen to the Dream Awareness Meditation. It will take you back to the heart quicker and will prepare you for exploration within the heart. Find a comfortable seat and listen to the full Dream Awareness Meditation that includes the Heart Awareness Meditation and exercise. When you are in the Dream Awareness Meditation, have gotten through the door into the white light space, begin to feel a deep desire to contact your future self. Through that deep desire a new door will appear that is much different from yours. Allow the door to open for your future self to appear. Allow your future self to present itself as it is. You'll find that surrendering to the experience is easy and your future self will happily show you who you are to become. Take in everything you're seeing and feeling. Step by step your future self will move closer towards you. Once you are face to face with your future self ask them one meaningful question about who they are. Allow yourself to receive the answer in which ever way it comes. Their door will suddenly appear and open. It's in this moment you will get a glimpse of what their world looks like. What do you see in their world? Take as long as you need to fully observe what's happening in their world. Your future self motions that your contact is over and makes their way back to their world. Slowly, step by step, make your way back to yourself, retracing through the Heart Awareness Meditation. Once you are back to your physical body take some time to write down your experiences.

The more you practice these meditations, you will start to see that meeting the future self is always an unexpected experience. The age may change every time, and the way the future self looks may change as well. The reason for the differences is the multitude of future selves that exist. It takes some time to train yourself to be comfortable with the feeling of contacting your future self. When you recognize the feeling, you can recall that feeling while in the space between to send a signal for the future self to arrive. Otherwise, a new future self will come each time until the recalling is learned. As you may have learned from doing the Dream Awareness Meditation, the future self seldom speaks. In that space, there is no use for words. The right brain has completely taken over, so the mode of communication is imagery and feeling. Those two modes alone can contain much more information than a few sentences. However, upon returning to the body, the brain will interpret the messages into language when the left brain comes back online and in control consciously. In the beginning, simple messages may remain that are like universal truths you may have heard before, but not incorporated into your conscious beliefs, such as, "everything is happening as it should" or "continue following your heart and trust it will lead you toward me". In my experience, the messages became progressively more intricate and detailed. The meeting of Amareld was very specific to me and carried meaning that I could consciously interpret, which may have been insignificant to someone else. The willingness to give these meditations time and practice will allow for more specific experiences of your own with your future self.

Successfully recalling a future self is something I like to call the Futurist Perspective. We will explore that in the next chapter.

The End of the Story

The story at the beginning of this chapter has more to it. It ends phenomenally. What I saw in that holographic screen was the future. When I experienced it at the time, I certainly didn't know. However, the next day, it came to fruition. I called my friend to come over and play music. When he arrived at my apartment, I buzzed him up, then picked up my guitar and sat down. Shortly after, my friend came into the apartment and sat down on the couch across from me. We chatted for a bit and began playing guitar. Suddenly, the realization dawned on me. It's happening. The experience I had the night before was happening. Each moment slowly slid by as I watched myself repeat what I had "envisioned". The uneasy feeling and the mumble of words were all there and happening. For a moment, I thought I would go back into the darkness, but I didn't. I remained, and my friend and I laughed at how strange I was acting.

I realized that it's a personal decision to meet the future self. The kind of experience I had when I was nineteen is seemingly exceptional. I not only "met" my future self, but I also had a direct visceral experience of being my future self, even if it was only one day into the future. That experience opened a portal into a perspective of how time and space work in a realm that is the antithesis of the physical reality we are attached to. I see the interconnection between that experience and the experience I had with Amareld, and the vision I had when I was eight years old of the white truck. Without the two events at eight and nineteen, I would not have met Amareld, and I would not have written this book. The ties that bind synchronicities are shaped and manifested within and without the heart. To adopt the Futurist Perspective is to have a heightened sense of those synchronicities.

Remember, life is a miracle masked by the mundane. To uncover the miracles is to accept the mundane as a resting point. That acceptance is a new perspective, and with a new perspective comes an advancement. With the heart's involvement, an acceleration occurs to advance more and more, bringing new perspectives regularly to give empowerment to the mundane. Your future self is eagerly waiting for you, anticipating the moment they can share with you all that is harmonious and beneficial for your life. They are there, deep within your heart. Trust brings harmony.

CHAPTER 6

Futurist Perspective

I stepped onto the elevator and pressed the silver button printed with the word "Roof". The elevator climbed quickly, and, in a manner of a few short moments, the elevator stopped smoothly and quietly as I reached my destination. The doors silently slid open, and a stream of blinding light burst into the gap. Shielding my eyes, I stepped through the threshold to behold the incredible sight before me. I dropped my arms to my side in awe. The rooftop was a forest, thick and wild, and it was teeming with life. Birds darted around, and their songs filled the humid air. I could only look around in astonishment.

Before me, a winding path led to a glass gazebo that overlooked the city surroundings. Seated inside on a simple patio chair was an old man. Looking closer, I immediately recognized him, so I walked along the path toward the gazebo. The old man didn't say a word; he simply stood up and smiled. He reached his hand out toward me and gently motioned for me to come closer. I walked up the few humble stairs into the gazebo and quietly stood next to him, but my heart was bursting. We looked out over the city sprawling in front of us. The sun's final light for the day surrounded the city in a vibrant golden yellow glow. We stood in silence. I looked at him and saw my eyes. He smiled, unwavering, and pointed to other rooftops. All the skyscrapers had forests adorning their crowns. It was his own endeavor. The building we were standing on top of was the first of his creations. He began an initiative to create forests on all skyscrapers.

We looked back at each other. A palpable warmth was exuding from him, a presence of serene contentment and surrender. Without a word spoken, I was given so much. He had been expecting me for a long time. He would come onto the roof and sit in the gazebo every day, knowing that I would show up one day and see what he sees. I looked at the sunset one last time to scan the horizon. Every building was green and living.

When I had the experience from the above story, I was awestruck. It had occurred during a guided meditation. The vision I had, took over, and my attention was not on the person guiding the meditation. As soon as the elevator door opened, I was completely taken by the experience. Seeing myself as an elderly man was beyond surreal, especially because of the presence I felt. The sense of reassurance was incredible. Knowing that there is a version of myself that has lived a purposeful life planted a seed within me. Was I interacting with my exact future self? Honestly, I don't know, but I am sure of one thing: I am sure that he is still helping me.

Unconsciously or consciously, we take ownership of ideas and thoughts. The perspective that streams through the mind can be taken as a personal insight to harness and utilize. Is that the whole truth? An idea gets labeled and possessed; all the while, a learned trait is developed and nurtured. A belief then surrounds the idea that its origin is undoubtedly from "me"— the personality and identity. Is that the whole truth? Asking these questions allows our curiosity to guide us toward the Futurist Perspective.

The Futurist Perspective is an ongoing influence. It is happening right now. There is a future self that is looking back to where you are right now. It is perhaps recollecting the memory of what you are doing right now that helped shape where they are in their life. It's a natural phenomenon that is quite normal. We look back on our past regularly; however, we often don't consider the full implication of what looking back can mean when it is a future version of ourselves looking back on us today.

Right now, your mentality, knowledge, and wisdom is a Futurist Perspective. In contrast to your past self, you have obtained an awareness of life that streams through your consciousness that remained untapped during your younger years. Likewise, there remains untapped knowledge and information for your present self that has been experienced by a future self. The question is which future self holds the kind of information that will truly lead you to fulfill your dreams? The path toward that future self is carved through the Futurist Perspective. There is a spontaneity that occurs as well. The future self that appears will not be what you expect. Take Amareld, for example. Synchronicity brought us together. My action of centering into my heart created an opening for her to stream through. Would she have come through if I didn't meditate before the kundalini class? Would she have come through if I didn't buy the harp and name it Amareld? Would she have come through if I didn't take up yoga and meditation many years before? I think it's obvious, not likely. Yet, with all the preparation I had done, there was no way of knowing in advance that she would come through as she did.

Doing the meditations and exercises builds trust. This trust brings harmony, and this sense of harmony is the future self that will be the most helpful and supportive. The goal of the future self is advancement. They want to see you succeed and become your truest and most exciting self. To get a sense of that purpose, it's necessary to look at your past self with that kind of nurturance. Be honest with yourself. Do you consistently look back at your past and encourage yourself that you'll become an amazing person? Do you recall when you were a teenager and give yourself grace for the choices you made that caused you embarrassment, disconnection, or shame, and remind yourself that it was all part of learning to be who you are today? Do you spend time with your child self and talk with them about how much you have learned and have grown into a heart-centered person? The answer for most people is no.

This last chapter will be of particular interest because even though we are discussing the Futurist Perspective, it has more to do with the past than it does the future. When we look to our future self, they are simultaneously looking at their past self. The power of healing comes from how we amend our past to integrate the energies into the heart so that more space is created for new insight and wisdom from the future self.

Advancement

Stop. Enjoy a deep breath. Inhale, fill your lungs completely. Exhale, empty your lungs completely. Feel in your heart, the best you can, it's great intelligence and wisdom connecting to future selves.

We hardly consider that we are advancing evolutionarily in daily life. Evolution is typically viewed on a large scale of thousands to millions of years, not personally in our short life span. We don't consider that our daily decisions can influence how we grow in a spiritual nature and how that can affect our future and ancestors. There are specific choices that determine how this evolution is taking place. Our daily decision making mainly involves interactions with the environment and material world. This is obvious and tangible. It is all around us and demanding our attention from the moment we open our eyes in the morning to when we close them at night. Many of us often fall asleep thinking of the issues and events of the material world. Our family is physical, our job is physical, the food we need to survive is physical, so we conclude life is physical. Although many of our choices are indeed based on this physical reality, there is still an evolution that can occur through meditation and meeting the future self, which will affect the physical world and how we interact with the environment. Imagine you meet someone you consider at the peak of their success and life. This person is someone you are inspired by and consider to be a great motivator. What does it feel like to be in that person's presence? It's exhilarating, isn't it? Meeting an inspirational figure is great; however, their goals aren't your goals. Their dreams aren't your dreams. To get a clear sense of the kind of evolution you want to experience, it's greatly profound to be face to face with your future self, who has accomplished precisely the dreams and goals you are working on. The evolution that happens in your heart's metaphysical space is a tangible feeling and experience since you see it both for yourself and as yourself.

The evolution into a version of yourself living a life of success, harmonious abundance, spiritual depth, and awareness is personal advancement. I use advancement rather than evolution here because there is a difference between the two words; advancement is more of a personal application, whereas evolution is involuntary or unconscious development. Consider your current self as Point A and your future self as Point B. In our common understanding of progressing through time to our future self, we think there is a lack of control when navigating toward a specific future self. For example, we may believe Point A is at twenty-eight years old, and Point B is at sixty-eight years old, and we will eventually become sixty-eight years old without knowing what kind of person we could become. I consider that as an unconscious evolution. However, with FLP, you can certainly know what kind of person you can potentially be at sixty-eight. With that kind of knowledge, we can advance to the wisdom of your sixty-eight-year-old self while still inhabiting your twenty-eight-year-old self. The relationship that has been developed with the intelligence of the heart allows the wisdom from the sixty-eight-year-old future self to be clearly and easily accepted and adopted. There isn't a limitation on continuing advancing, either. The expanse of time, even through thousands of years, can be shortened. This understanding isn't new at all. Yogic practitioners from India, Tibet, Africa, China, and other neighboring countries share the wisdom that the soul/spirit or consciousness is not limited to the aging body. Consciousness can advance through time faster than the physical body, benefit from the greater energetic capacities from the future time lines, and depart that energy through the body of the current and present time line the consciousness originated from. Paramahansa Yogananda expresses this truth in his book *The Autobiography of a Yogi*:

"One thousand Kriyas practiced in 8.5 hours gives the yogi, in one day, the equivalent of one thousand years of natural evolution: 365,000 years of evolution in one year. In three years, a Kriya Yogi can thus accomplish by intelligent self-effort the same result that nature brings to pass in a million years" (Yogananda 1946, 210).

There is a stark difference between looking into one's future by forty years and what Yogananda stated regarding the power of Kriya Yoga. However, this written source provides evidence of the capabilities we have as humans and as advanced beings. To advance ourselves beyond what our senses and their perceptions allow is, in truth, a natural phenomenon. To experience that phenomenon, as Yogananda says, it takes intelligent self-effort. It's not entirely evident in the quote from Yogananda; however, the intelligent self-effort is not an egoic will power but an action from the heart. As awareness is applied to the heart, paired with techniques, such as Kriya Yoga in Yogananda's case, or FLP, consciousness expands as it is no longer confined to the body by limited egoic structures of identity and its encompassing material world. The appeal of desire changes. The desires from one's personality are transmuted to desires that continue the process of expansion and advancement.

The result is a change in character. How those changes look is unique to each of us. They can be changes in food, clothing, speech mannerism, location of living, sexual orientation, and attitude toward politics and the world's social norms. It's important to realize that the advancement that occurs is an additive. Whatever seems to be "taken away", such as friends, jobs, relationships, or whatever is meaningful at that time, makes room for new experiences and more life that reflects the expansive consciousness that is flowing more freely. The changes are not completely out of your control. It's noticeable that the occurring advancement is inspiring great change. Remember, the utilization of the Futurist Perspective is a harmonious adoption—what seems to "fall away" will do so gracefully. Typically, people who do not like the changes you are making will want to keep you at the level they are comfortable with. However, their desire for you to remain as the image they hold in their mind is outdated, and it's important to educate the people around you of the more advanced you that is blossoming. You can use the conviction of your belief in your future self to inspire your friends to support the new facets of your self-exploration. You have advanced toward a future self with a perspective of greater harmony and integration. Your future self wants to happily connect with you. Think of the connection with your future self as a way to link your desires with their desires. That link will help maintain a stronger connection that leads you more closely to their way of living. All of this is part of the process.

Recall in chapter 2 when I briefly mentioned the water filled fascia that surrounds the heart. I cannot say with 100% accuracy that the following insight is without a doubt how the fascia functions in accordance with the heart. However, with any scientific theory there is a period of time needed to find as much information necessary to indicate that indeed there is merit to the proposed claims. Knowing now that your current heart is in continual communication with your past heart, and your future heart it can be concluded that there is a specific mechanism to allow for the communication to take place in the physical realm. As the heart beats, that pulse vibrates the water droplets that are suspended on the fibers of the fascia around the heart. The water droplets act as magnifiers and harmonizers as the heart wave pulse surrounds the body. We now know that experiments have taken place by Masaru Emoto that indicate the possibility that water has some kind of memory. Though the experiments aren't completely conclusive, I want to take the idea one step further anyways to help formulate how our own fascia filled water can complete the picture. The electro-magnetic waves emanating from the heart contains information of our daily experiences . As the wave passes through the water in the fascia the water captures the information and stores it in the fascia throughout the body. With the body going through this exchange at all times there is an unbroken link through the heart, water filled fascia, and body that extends through time. Your heart when you were five years old and it's memories stored in the fascia is still in your heart now. Your heart now that is beating and taking account of what's occurring in real time is recollected as a past moment from your future self. Finally, your future self that is looking back at you right now is filling the room with it's heart wave pulses as the interconnection between all hearts supersede time through the water barrier around the heart. Take a moment right now to focus on the barrier of water around your heart. feel how the heart is pulsing information into it. Feel how the heart waves are amplified and magnified through the water and harmonized with your nervous system. And feel your life force around your body. All of that energy contains all the information of who you were, who you are, and who you will become, and beyond. This is the Akashic Record.

Recapitulation

Looking back at the past must be done with awareness. Included within the awareness must be felt qualities of honor, compassion, respect, and upliftment. These qualities are absolutely necessary because deliberately affecting the past memories will result in the effect of integration between your past self and current self. Focusing on these aspects encourages a harmonious connection.

There is a societal development with regards to specific beliefs surrounding the past and future. When we look to the future, there are one of two experiences: a black emptiness veils our vision to only be clouded with either vague ideas of unknowing, or vague ideas of knowing, both of our own creation or imagination, or influenced from an outside source. We may desire to know the future but find ourselves dismissing the idea as foolish. As we look into the past, the memories are seldom clear or accurate, and perhaps just informative enough to allow for the simple acknowledgment that they are either good or bad memories. Numerous studies show that how we remember the past is heavily altered by time and perspective. At times, we conjure strong urges and desires to change the past, yet we say to ourselves, "It's impossible."

Why? Why are these beliefs adopted?

Healing is a multidimensional experience and methodology. The past and future are not exempt from that healing. Looking into the past for relief is not only possible, but it is also necessary. Looking into the future for clarity and justification is not only necessary; it is fundamental. The wholeness of your personal expression is not a confined body that must endure the mundane routines and rituals of present moment personal survival. It is an expansive library of wisdom that grants access to a totality of expression through a multitude of faculties. The past and the future are fully part of those faculties.

Within the content of stored memories are contained Futurist Perspectives. Lost in the plentitude of daily stored memories, the Futurist Perspectives are gems waiting to be unearthed and polished. Finding the Futurist Perspectives is a journey and endeavor just as finding a raw gemstone in the earth and polishing it to a brilliant luster. This polishing is the process of Recapitulation. When centered in the heart, the negative beliefs and doubts vanish, and the ability to recognize memories through the heart amplifies. The result is a vision projected through the heart similar to how one might play out a scene in the mind's eye within the brain; however, it is lively and animated in a near physical experience. This process is similar to Retrieval; however, the heart draws the Futurist Perspective from memory. The heart finds the wisdom in the past event to reassure you that growth is always possible even in the darkest of times.

The Futurist Perspectives gained through Recapitulation allow integration to occur, enabling the subconscious to utilize Recapitulation instantaneously in daily life. The practice of finding wisdom in past memories empowers the ability to find wisdom in current, real-time situations. Learning from the past now has a whole new meaning. The past and future are deeply interconnected to the present. Even as you read this now, your future self is energetically connected to your focus and concentration. Their own focus and concentration are encoded with wisdom and knowledge imprinted through your present moment consciousness. The more the heart is involved and incorporated into focus, concentration, and feeling, the more the wisdom can be downloaded purposely as the future self's perspective is observed and known. Thus, the Futurist Perspective is within everything that makes up your experience, as your future self was once there and has the full capability of sending wisdom back to you, filling the entire space you are in right now with wisdom and heart intelligence.

Let us explore the process of Recapitulation to find the Futurist Perspective by examining the earlier chapters of this book. This exercise will develop a new skill of raising awareness of what the Futurist Perspectives are in your life. Take the examples below with a grain of salt and think critically about your personal experiences. It's OK to disagree. You may find better examples that speak to you, and that is perfectly fine. This next section focuses on application and practice in conscious recognition of the Futurist Perspective. I encourage you to take your broadened understanding and skim each chapter again over the coming weeks. You will begin to see evidence of the Futurist Perspective not only within this book but as you are now being guided forward, in yourself and in your experiences in the world as well.

Chapter 1:

"Can the left brain take on a subconscious role of operation and the right brain take on a conscious role? Yes, they certainly can. However, the function of the left and right brain hemispheres change. That change can be attributed to an added component that is necessary for the neutralization to occur."

What makes this quote a Futurist Perspective? When I considered the information from the above quote, I first realized that it wasn't in any literature that I've read or studied. It's quite particular, and that uniqueness is something that I utilized when I continued to contemplate what it meant to experience a role reversal of the brain hemispheres. Once I had the experience of a silent and thoughtless mind while simultaneously witnessing vivid images and scenes, it became clear that the initial information of reversing the brain hemispheres had originated from somewhere beyond my current self. I had tapped into the flow of energy from a future self who had the experience and working knowledge of reversing the hemispheres.

Do you agree with the perspective above? Is it enough to claim that reversing the roles of the brain hemispheres is true from personal experiences? Reread Chapter 1 and find what you would consider a Futurist Perspective. Then look back through your day and consider an event that could hold a Futurist Perspective.

Chapter 2:

"Within expression, there is a natural tendency for feeling and heartfelt emotion. That's not to say expression lacks logic. On the contrary, logic and reasoning are supported by heartfelt emotion. What can occur with the coordination of the seemingly contradictory concepts is a more impactful speech and portrayal of the ideas being expressed. The result is an experience greater than simply hearing words. Expression is a cause for stimulation throughout the body. It can respond with a rush of sensation that flushes through the skin to clearly indicate impactful truth or perhaps causes our eyes to be literally flooded from the power of honest expression. There are various ways to observe how the physical self aligns with true heartfelt emotion and expression."

What makes this quote a Futurist Perspective? The tangible feeling of sensation flushing through the skin and the inspiration to express through feeling are synchronistic elements of an inclusion of the heart's intelligence. The heart is a gateway for the future self to have access to the present self, and the energetic information streaming from the future self aligns with the synchronistic elements. The mistake usually made when expressing through the heart is taking ownership. Though the information is coming from a future self, the use of "my" and "mine" blocks awareness of where the information is coming from. If the future self isn't considered, how can the heart be considered?

Do you agree with the perspective above? Can the future self interact with the present self energetically? Considering all the information in the book, it seems likely. Blockages to phenomenal experiences are our own creations. Shifting the perspective of the experience from phenomenal to normal is a personal choice. Regularly interacting with your future self in real-time can be normal. Reread Chapter 2 and find what you would consider a Futurist Perspective, then look back through your day and consider an event that could hold a Futurist Perspective.

Chapter 3:

"Merging is the necessary action to allow entry to the 'empty space' of a nonphysical existence through the heart. In this space, a realm can be experienced that opens a portal to the future self... Over time with a dedicated practice, our current physical sense of consciousness merges with our greater eternal and expansive consciousness: the future self."

What makes this quote a Futurist Perspective? When was the last time you casually heard anyone say there is a portal in the heart; moreover, the ability to enter the portal and travel to an inner location where the future self appears? The spiritual functions of the heart are a nuance. Their navigation methods arise through the heart itself, which means that learning how to navigate the spiritual functions of the heart must come from inner wisdom. From within comes awareness that all hearts are interconnected. The portal is likened to the veins and ventricles that allow blood to carry oxygen throughout the body. Like the veins and ventricles, as long as the heart is working and pumping, openness is available for flow. The portal is always available to flow from one heart to the other toward the future self.

Do you agree with the perspective above? Is there a portal within the heart that links all past, present, and future selves? When trust in the heart's intelligence is normalized, its abilities are known easily and harmoniously. Reread Chapter 3 and find what you would consider a Futurist Perspective, then look back through your day and consider an event that could hold a Futurist Perspective.

Chapter 4:

"Fragmentation is a multi-faceted experience of separation. It occurs physically, mentally, emotionally, and spiritually. The first experience of fragmentation is through consciousness; the transition from nonphysical to physical life. However, it's not the exact moment of complete physicality. The second experience of fragmentation from wholeness is birth."

What makes this quote a Futurist Perspective? Further into the future, the idea of contacting future selves is less and less obscure. Not only will individuals contact their current life future selves, but they will also contact future lives beyond their current life. Information regarding life after death will be understood and experienced without physical death. Beyond this lies future selves who observe the process of fragmentation through a potent state of consciousness. The way consciousness turns physical can be perceived and witnessed from this state of consciousness until the intention and desire of birth shifts awareness from the nonphysical existence to physical existence.

Do you agree with the perspective above? What beliefs arise regarding personal identity when considering a nonphysical existence? Reread Chapter 4 and find what you would consider a Futurist Perspective, then look back through your day and consider an event that could hold a Futurist Perspective.

Chapter 5:

"A nonphysical reality is inconceivable. We cannot comprehend it through theory or explanation. It must simply be experienced. The experience we have as our natural physical self is a hint to what can be experienced as its antithesis; however, any direct searching for the complete antithesis is a cyclic loop of illusion. It is an exercise in futility while in the non-meditative waking state of left-brain consciousness. The process of FLP is a potentiated shift of perspective to allow for the nonphysical realm of existence to be a forefront realization through the heart's intelligence and clear, intuitive communication via the right brain."

What makes this quote a Futurist Perspective? The heart is the key to re-entering the nonphysical realm of existence with awareness and alertness. This is constantly being told to us from the heart. It's being spoken to us through the language of the heart. Now it's time to listen and receive the guidance to continue deeper toward our true nature.

Do you agree with the perspective above? Is it so challenging to enter the heart and allow it to show you its intelligence and the ever-expansive world? Read Chapter 5 again, and find what you would consider a Futurist Perspective, then look back through your day and consider an event that could hold within it a Futurist Perspective.

It's perfectly fine to make mistakes. It's perfectly fine to practice these meditations daily and still experience what you would consider to be "failures" as you learn, gain new awareness, and question your beliefs and ideas about your evolution over your life. With more practice and experience, you will begin to see these failures as necessary stepping stones. The point of this book is to open a door into the heart. Just because we gain a new understanding and knowledge about spiritual advancement doesn't mean life magically gets easier, and that entering the heart will unveil all the secrets to life. Entering the heart and expanding within it begins a new, lifelong pursuit and practice of surrendering. It's challenging. The immensity of this process is precisely what makes it so great. I use a canyon as an obstacle in Heart Awareness Meditation to represent the understanding of this process. We are suddenly faced with the big picture. However, we overcome the canyon one step at a time. It is a responsibility of mine to emphasize that the future self is not a new age gimmick about predicting the future. This book isn't about predicting the future. This book is about getting to know yourself in unique and creative ways, and to know that you exist so incredibly, that reality itself has been waiting to show you what happens when you choose to go deep within your heart and expand.

Most importantly, the future can still be exciting and a mystery. Getting in touch with a future self doesn't suddenly remove the mystery of who you'll become. Getting in touch with your future self adds to your confidence that you can face the mystery with courage and know that you are supported by a heart that connects to not only your past and future selves, but to everyone on Earth. Your future self is with you now, and everything in this book has taught you to be with your future self, as well.

Tessa's Personal FLP Experience

I met Zorananda before I started doing mental health work in my life to discover and process the trauma I had experienced as a child and teenager. These traumas were aspects of my life that were separate pieces of my identity, and learning the terms and ideas like fragmentation and merging helped me to look back on the healing process of my history and understand it from not only a logical and psychological standpoint but from a spiritual standpoint as well. The process of learning to live through a Futurist Perspective parallels so closely with the traditional healing work of trauma, and being able to access it through the heart when trauma experiences are so wrought with anxiety and dissociation helps me to stay present and trust that beauty will come from it. Understanding what I know now about the Futurist Perspective, I can see how clearly I could take the pain of my past and have the energy of shame and fear, and re-integrate these parts into who I would become, with the guidance of my future self.

One of the most impactful experiences I have had with my future self was very spontaneous. I had been meditating by going into my heart on and off for months but was never disciplined. However, I believe it's OK to be imperfect, and that the Universe will come to meet us exactly as it intends. A lot of the pain I experienced from trauma had created unconscious beliefs that my needs, safety, and worth came from everything outside of me. Just before my future self came through, I had been in an experience where I was quite emotionally vulnerable with a very important person to me. I had expressed an invitation toward them to create more connection and share more spiritual practices, similar to how religious people pray together, but in a way that resonated with us. Not only did they not acknowledge or recognize the significance of the invitation, but they also dismissed me by changing the subject and left shortly after, totally oblivious.

I felt so ashamed, foolish, and worthless for extending myself and sharing my dream with them and being rejected, all in an instance. It was overwhelming and triggering, and my body immediately went into a panic attack. I was shivering and holding myself on my sofa as my body processed the sudden rush of cortisol and adrenaline, crying and unable to breathe properly. Usually, in panic attacks, I try to do whatever I can to get through it until my body relaxes enough to start using logic again. However, this time, as I was cycling through emotional pain and self-destructive urges, my mind cleared very abruptly and I was able to breathe again. I felt an immense and beautiful peace bloom inside me and spread throughout my entire body and beyond; I was no longer aware of the physical room around me. I saw myself older but not by much, confident, standing up tall, but relaxed, long hair falling behind me (I had short hair at the time), and I radiated what I would describe as wholeness. I smiled at myself as I held my hands to my chest, and then gracefully pushed them outwards toward me. I felt like I was hit by a truck in the best way. I came back to my body and physical senses very suddenly, and a great feeling of love and acceptance spread throughout my entire being. For days afterward, I was processing this sudden feeling of compassion that struck me. A version of me in the future looked at me and didn't see someone who was abandoned and worthless; they were proud of their past self for taking a risk and asking for what they needed. Even more, what they revealed to me was that I didn't need to share this practice of deepening spirituality for it to have meaning and significance and that the intimacy I crave will always be available within me.

Having this visceral experience began the journey of true self-respect, self-worth, and learning to live by my values, regardless of the people around me who do or don't want to join in. I am very excited that my future self is someone who goes her own way, unshaken by the opinions of people around her, and I feel encouraged knowing this is what I am moving forward to every day. FLP and the disciplines and attitudes shared have certainly helped me trust my inner guide more and be open to the future not being what I envisioned, but something even greater than I could have hoped for.

PART 3

CHAPTER 7

Mystical Rhythms

Have you noticed that intuition comes and goes? There is an ebb and flow because intuition is a wave. There are small waves, medium waves, and large waves, one no more significant than the other, though noticeably different with intensity. The intimate and conscious relationship with the heart allows for greater sensitivity to the movement of the waves, the mystical rhythms. There is information in the waves. In a synchronized nature, the rise of the waves inspires a reaction. Corresponding to the inspiration is usually some kind of event, either in the experiences of the outer world, or the inner sanctum of personality and patterns.

When intuition arises, a deliberate focus on the heart is paired with and present to reality. The information from the waves of the intuition can be viewed and learned from. What allows the interpretation of the intuitive information? While the focus on the heart allows access to the intuitive information, the language of the heart allows for comprehension of the wisdom within the intuitive information. Comprehension is very important. Think of hearing a language you cannot comprehend. The person speaking the language could impart great wisdom, yet you will not benefit from the given wisdom. Until you learn the language, its words are empty of significance and personal meaning. Once you realize that the heart has its own language and relearn it, the intuitive information will be understood. Now, with the comprehendible intuitive information, how you act changes.

Our actions are driven by information. The knowledge we hold onto about life and how to live in a society comes from the *putting in motion* of information. That putting in motion has been learned over time and gathered to form a picture of ourselves that is ideal and can function appropriately enough to achieve the plans and goals that shape the rest of our lives. The waves of the intuitive information bring guidance for those plans and goals.

There is a natural complexity surrounding the timing of the intuitive information. The complexity comes from the relationship between our *awake* rational thinking and the random occurrence of the intuitive information. The relationship is a necessary, natural disconnect due to the compartmentalized function of the left brain, where only one intuitive sense arises at a time. The intuitive senses before and after remain in the subconscious so as not to conflate the intuitive information within the compartmentalizing left brain in the awake state. That conflation already happens in the subconscious where there is no compartmentalization. The rational mind can only deal with the present, sudden intuition. However, the heart innately processes and knows that the intuitive waves are never ceasing. The time interval doesn't matter, in the sense that the function of producing waves automatically induces and endures perpetuity. The nature of the waves is to have a pulse. With every pulse of the wave, there is an arising of intuitive information that can be significant and intercepted or subverted to the subconscious. Which is more advantageous, only receiving intuitive information spontaneously and incomprehensibly or information that is anticipated and clearly processed? Obviously, the latter. The key here is to find in the body what parallels a perpetual rhythm and enduring pulse. I'm sure you can figure that out on your own.

Follow the rhythm. When you listen to music and shivers crawl over your skin, the music is taken in by more than the sound traveling through the ears, especially when the lyrics are impactful and influential, and the rhythm is powerful and much easier to *get into*. The key is feeling and surrendering. The personally meaningful lyrics, the tone of the music, and the overall enjoyment unravel the synchronicity of deeply feeling the music while tapping into the heart. The *all-encompassing* subconscious that pervades our conscious mind is not so hidden as first perceived. The very embrace of the heart and its realm (the subconscious) is unveiled. Just as the rational thinking mind communicates through language, the creative mind communicates through feeling, imaging, and expressing.

Remember the "natural disconnect" mentioned earlier? With the involvement of the heart and communicating through creative feeling awareness, an ever-present connection becomes realized. The right brain becomes energized as more blood flow enters by means of diversion from the left brain. The visual and feeling based faculties of the right brain become more vivid and clear to comprehend. The connections allow for a perceptible transference of guidance from the heart. Thus, the mystical rhythms form the basis of resonance and harmony. The heart has our best interests in mind. With the heart's continual conscious presence, the rhythm of its pulse can more easily and readily bring information to act on. It's suddenly not so difficult to *follow your intuition*. The oncoming intuitive information opens the door to the heart from the inside. We cannot help but act from the heart when leading to its door is normalized often. Its realm of empathy, compassion, and unconditional love naturally encodes our intuition-led actions with goodness.

Imagine a situation where there is subtle guidance, a gut feeling. Pause, breathe in deeply, close your eyes and exhale, sending your focus into the heart with the exhale. Move through the open door of the heart where the intuition has risen out of. With consistent practice, the door remains open, and the intuitive information is a welcomed guest, building a home within the heart's space. How your inner sanctum and home is built is a cooperative endeavor between you and the intuitive information. From internal to external, the heart and its intuitive information are the driving force for life decisions to replicate the inner heart space's serenity.

The future self has a hand in offering guidance regarding life decisions, whether we are aware or not. When the door in the heart opens, and the wave of intuition rises into our perception, the future self can stream into the intuitive information to inspire you to act toward manifesting that future self as a present-day reality. The whole point of this work is to become conscious of this process so that *you can choose the future self.* Because why would you want guidance from a future self who is sabotaging you?

The amount of processing that occurs in the body is overwhelming and happens entirely in a single moment. The natural filter is a definite safety mechanism to the compartmentalizing left brain. When we look into the past, the memories only allow a limited amount of information through recall. That is because we are using the left brain present functioning to remember the parts of the memory that are relevant to the circumstances in the outer world. It makes sense that the future as an actuality is more limited. Like I said in Chapter 1, the difference between the past and future selves is feeling. Once out of the limiting grip of the left brain and into the heart's realm, there is a perpetual feeling without good and bad judgment. The flow of feeling is moved and integrated. With complete access to the heart's intuitive information, the calling upon the future self is clearly actualized. Feeling is the driving force into more clarity and vivid imagery. The future self has a felt sense of intuition to recall the past moment of your present self, reaching for the future self. Because your future self has spent many years from the time of your present self, the ability to manifest as an influence is much easier and synchronously available. This process is done through the right brain, and there isn't any learning process through verbalization. The left brain is silent; thus, the future self's influence is through action, following the intuition, and seeing trough to harmonious decisions.

We do this frequently when we look into the past at regrettable decisions. "I wish I didn't do that." There is a want to allow our current presence to appear somehow in the past and inspire a change for a different outcome. However, the feeling of regret and focus on the negative past event is a package of information sent to the past self that maintains the cycle of feeling regret. In the past, we weren't aware that there is an overarching connection between the past, present, and future, so it seems like the future self doesn't have an effect. In this very book are the philosophies, hypotheses, theories, and practices to redevelop the connection between the brain and heart. When we make the decision to connect into the heart and reach out to a future self, we invite, through synchronicity, the future self to look back at the present moment and offer its presence of greater knowledge, love, empathy, compassion, and wisdom. Because in that very moment, your future self has also connected to their (your) heart and has reached out to you, creating a bridge between hearts to communicate beneficial information.

The Futurist Perspective is derived from this process. The presence of your future self is the sudden wisdom observed in your current environment. Can you feel it? Look around you. The wisdom is in everything. Do you honestly think there is only one future self looking back at you now? How many times have you looked back at one specific memory? Just because it seems like each time has happened independent of the other, your past self is influenced by each one at that moment. However, the current self can only handle one at a time. This is important to understand in regards to the power of the heart.

My hypothesis is that in the present moment, we not only have influences from the present world, but there are also influences from the past selves and their patterns *and* future selves. Not all future selves are helpful. Some future selves have chosen a destructive path, while others have chosen a more uplifting and harmonious path. When we are disconnected from the heart, it's fair game for all future selves to extend their influence. By remaining ignorant, we don't know which future self's influence is coming through. We simply take ownership of the information and guidance and fall victim to the overwhelming force that exhausts our attempts to grasp it all.

By involving the heart, we see where the influence to act comes from. The decision to act on guidance and communication from a harmonious future self is obvious and anticipated. There is no longer pressure from the overwhelming force. *Entering the heart releases the pressure.* Following the guidance of the harmonious future self is the foundation of following the mystical rhythms, a total experience of pulsating intuitive heart waves, crafting synchronicities to co-operate with the future self. More and more synchronicities are placed along the road of life to blossom like a flower, the song of harmony with the beneficial future self.

The conscious journey into and with the heart is an uncovering of who you truly are. The initial fear of the heart's depth is a step toward the uncovering. It's challenging because the fear of entering the heart seems like a warning. The warning is an illusion to cover the door into the heart. When closing the eyes, the darkness and its strange vastness are intimidating. The swell of thoughts and feelings can be confusing, which is the perfect distraction away from the heart. There is a needed trust to know the heart can provide guidance. Remember, trust brings harmony. How to trust is to apply exercises. As you have learned in this book, the exercises directly apply harmony through your own practice and connection with the heart. When there is a medium between decision and focus on the heart, trust is an actualization. The need for trust is a personal embodiment for harmony to strengthen and adhere to bonds between your heart and identity.

The disconnection provides synchronicity to abide by the fear. We all experience this disconnect, and the best way to ease the fear is to help each other; to remind ourselves and each other that our hearts are powerful. Together, we can ease the discomfort of trusting each other because we individually trust our own hearts. What I foresee is group meditation becoming a social norm where people meditate together like meeting to play a sport. A new comradery is forming. The more we connect deeply with our hearts and come together to connect to each other's hearts, the more we merge with one another to amplify a large presence of empathy, compassion, unconditional love, and acceptance. A new sense of freedom is emerging that to be in the heart's realm is an unburdened experience; we all have access to participate in the great expanse of intuitively guided intelligence and love. It's all happening, and it's time to enter our hearts to witness it and be it.

The mystical rhythm is an innate feature that is present within all of us and nature equally. All of nature creates sound. From the inanimate rushing river, the rocks tumbling down a mountainside, the nearly inaudible clicking of bugs and their loud buzzing, to the mating calls of animals, all of nature is frequently and perpetually a musical cacophony of pure creation. Then there is humanity and its variety of languages. What makes us special is our ability to produce language in the silent confines of the mind. The strange inner world is so well hidden from the outside world yet can be loud and distracting. We fail to grasp that the random and erratic mental chattering is the babbling river of the mystical rhythm. When we learn to see the visions and verbal manifestation as the flow and rhythm of our own energetic input and output, a very real geometry becomes apparent. Either the geometry is chaotic or formed purposefully to concentrate the mystical rhythm's very power. This is the secret of musical masterpieces. When we listen to enchanting and awe-inspiring music, its linear expression seems flat with a beginning and an end. However, there is a hidden geometry, and what was once seemingly linear is a coalescing, spiraling, pulsating form producing a realm of experience. You are the greatest musical masterpiece. Within you is a pulsating form that gives life to an entire realm of existence that can expand into infinite realms beyond physicality.

As long as it remains confined to our skull's small diameter, the mystical rhythm will appear insignificant when in truth, the mystical rhythm cannot be contained for it is in all things and of all things. However, our thought process is the direct source of misdirection, deceiving and confusing any rationale that there is *something* beyond personal identity and human nature. Our obsession with materialism is largely remedied by experiencing the mystical rhythm within a very real part of our sense of self. Once the mystical rhythm is clearly defined, it becomes obvious that our entire experience of the outside world has been influenced by something so fundamental yet problematic to society at large.

Dimethyl Triptomine

This section of the book will most likely be considered the most controversial. Dimethyl Triptomine (DMT) is largely illegal in most parts of the world, except for Brazil because of ayahuasca. The Brazilian government has protected ayahuasca because of its cultural importance within Indigenous communities. DMT is an active component within ayahuasca and produces the psychedelic visions within the experience. What makes DMT so controversial is its position as a scheduled controlled substance in North America. Luckily, speaking about DMT and its effects is becoming less taboo because of a handful of forerunners like Rick Strassman, Terence and Dennis McKenna, and Duncan Trussell.

My intention here is to share my experiences with DMT in a way that will help tie the theme of synchronicity together within this book. I find it unlikely that, as a reader, you had the slightest clue that each chapter had a hidden element of DMT within it. Similarly, I assume you haven't the slightest clue that, in fact, we all have a small amount of DMT within us, circulating in our bloodstreams. To be clear, this final section is more about my personal experiences and less about the science and chemical nature of DMT. If you do want to learn more about the science of DMT, please read *DMT: The Spirit Molecule* by Rick Strassman. However, I do have a hypothesis that I am slowing turning into a theory, which I will unveil at the end.

Finally, before I go into my experiences, I need to state a disclaimer: I am in no way suggesting or recommending you to try DMT. The point of my accounts here are to more deeply relate to the power of the heart, and how the realm of DMT is accessible through the meditations detailed in this book. My experiences with DMT and psychedelics are few, and my experiences of the heart's realm through meditation are far more in number. Please be safe, and trust that you have the tools within you to expand the great intelligence, compassion, and empathy within your heart.

Synchronicity of Krishna: Fruition of a Dream

I was standing in front of my childhood townhome, looking up to the sky. The sky was wonderfully blue and completely clear; there wasn't a cloud in sight. I was marveling at how vibrant everything around me was. The grass was brilliantly green, the townhomes were sharp and radiant, and the sun was not a sun at all. My feeling of wonder and brilliance turned to confusion and curiosity. In place of the sun was Krishna. He was golden with several thin circular rings revolving around him. He was in a cross-legged posture with all six arms moving slowly up and down, bent at the elbows, each holding an object. The sky suddenly turned pitch-black, yet I could see the grass all around me and the townhomes as if it were still midday. I noticed ever so carefully that the blue sky was still there as well, over-lapped with the pitch-black sky. When I closed my right eye, suddenly, the whole sky was blue, and when I closed my left eye, the whole sky was black. I blinked back and forth, switching between seeing a blue and black sky. When I looked at Krishna again, he seemed to be amused by my sudden realization. This whole time I was standing in one place. The dream had no movement, but suddenly, I began to move and walk past the townhomes. The grassy ground started to slope and turn into a gentle hill. I walked up the grassy hill, still with Krishna in view, but not knowing at all what could be on the other side of the hill. As I reached the top of the hill, I heard very peculiar music. It didn't have any organized rhythm or melody; it was mainly a cacophony of clanking chimes and bells and vocal chanting. I saw a sea of people wearing white robes. There was a man close in front of me sitting in the grass. I walked up to him and asked, "Is this a Hare Krishna parade?"

The man looked up at me and said plainly, "Yes, it is."

I woke up from the dream feeling a bit confused, but more so intrigued by how lucid the dream was while still not being in control at all. Why was Krishna in place of the sun? Why was the sky blue and black? Why did I stumble upon a Hare Krishna parade? At least to me, there was an intelligence at work that was weaving Krishna as a theme from my dream life to my real life.

I had this dream while living with my brother Adam when I was twenty. Though I'm not entirely sure exactly what month it was when I had the dream, I know that this next part happened during the summer, and it was not a dream.

My good friend Kris was a contender in a skateboard competition in Calgary, and a few of us tagged along to watch him compete. Kris is an amazing skater. In fact, we all grew up skateboarding together, and as each of us strayed away from skating, Kris maintained his passion and love for the complexity and challenge of skateboarding. When we arrived in Calgary, the weather was beautiful. The wind was calm with a slight breeze, and the sky was completely clear and bright blue.

We had some time before Kris competed, so we went downtown to stroll around and hang out. As we were walking down the street, I could hear some music playing. Just as we got to the intersection, the music became much louder and obviously clear. We walked right into a Hare Krishna parade! I immediately remembered my dream of seeing Krishna and the parade and began laughing out loud. I told my friends about the dream, and we all laughed at how ridiculous it is that I would have a dream about a Hare Krishna parade. I was the one in my friend group known to have prophetic dreams, and instead of it being overly weird and strange, it was accepted and somewhat celebrated. I'm very grateful that I have people in my life who know how strange I am at times, especially when it comes to my dreams, and find it to be quite normal because of how well I handle the fruition of some dreams in real life.

Several years later, I moved into Sunbelly. By meeting people through synchronicity and the conscious community in Edmonton, a few of my housemates and I were invited to experience DMT. At this point, I have had several psychedelic journeys with psilocybin, LSD, and MDMA, and it felt to me that DMT was the precipice of my psychedelic adventures. I was nervous, and I didn't know what to expect. I had a thorough understanding of how DMT works from reading Rick Strassman's book, but reading about a highly psychedelic substance is never enough to truly gauge what kind of experience will manifest.

The day had arrived for us all to embark on the internal journey of psychedelic self-discovery. It was a special occasion because we were all doing DMT for the first time. Our friend, who organized the journey, was the only one familiar with the substance, and we found comfort in knowing that she felt confident in her role as a supportive guide in creating a safe container for the journey. That is very important. Set and setting are crucial, especially because of how immediately intense DMT is. There isn't gradual arousal that eases the body and mind into a new realm. Nearly upon intake will the process begin to turn into a kaleidoscopic spiral of geometries, patterns, sounds, voices, along with a deep sense of overwhelming surrender into a space utterly unknown to the predominant physically oriented mind. To have someone sober who can ensure that everything is OK and have a thoroughly comfortable space makes for a great experience of the spirit molecule.

I happily stepped up to be the first to take the plunge, so to speak, though underneath that happy facade was a bone-shivering nervousness. I was assured that I'd be totally fine, that the substance was not harmful at all, and that I was completely supported by everyone present. Our method of drawing the smoke from the burning DMT was crude, to say the least, but it was effective. In one large pull, I inhaled the entire volume of smoke into my lungs. The smoke was surprisingly hot, and I could feel my throat slightly burn. I did as I was requested and held the smoke as long as possible.

The alteration of all I knew of reality began. I couldn't hold the smoke any longer as my body began to tingle and numb simultaneously. I was almost losing the function of controlling any movement, yet I was fully capable of moving. In the fabric of the room, just in front of me, nodes of spiral fractals began to appear and twist. With each twist, the nodes began to emanate a pulsing array of colors from blue, purple, red, and green. I was sitting cross-legged, and when I looked around at the room and at my friends, I couldn't help but smile and laugh at what I was seeing. Upon closing my eyes for a moment, I could see a ball of golden light at the base of my spine. Suddenly, I felt a strong pressure right where the ball of light was, and my pelvis locked into place. The light shot up my spine and out my eyes. As I opened my eyes when the light shined forward, a large golden-white portal was in front of me. At that moment, Krishna stepped out from the portal. I could hear, see, smell, and feel the entire presence of Krishna. I could hear the jangling of bells and voices chanting incoherent mantras, I could see their many arms with instruments and other objects, and I could smell sweet, strong incense. The vision in front of me, and the total experience of Krishna was wonderfully ecstatic. I remembered suddenly that I was sitting on the bed in front of my friends, and the vision disappeared. I could feel each person's emotional states. One friend was calm and serene, two other friends were a bit worried and fearful, and our guide was softly telling me to lay down. I looked at her, in bewilderment because her lips weren't moving and I could hear her repeat, in my mind "Lay down. Lay down. Just lay down. Lay DOWN. LAY DOWN!" Each time she said it, her voice became increasingly more intense until I just couldn't fight it anymore. I laid down.

The journey changed dramatically. I was suddenly in a dark room with a red light. I was sitting in a chair. It took me a few moments to realize where I was. I was in the opening scene of the movie *Logan's Run*. It was surreal. I was completely submerged in the scene. I looked around, got up from the chair, and touched the walls. Everything felt so real. Just like in the movie, there was a voice that was communicating with me. Only it was a male voice, and the voice was sharing some shocking revelations with me.

"This room represents your brain. Everything you consume through visual and audio media shapes the malleable form of your brain. Be careful about what you watch and what you listen to. Look around. All of this has been implanted in your brain. Everything about a Hollywood movie is designed to be implanted and direct how you feel and think about your way of life. The scene, the actors, the lighting, the music, the way the scenes are edited, the camera angles, the dialogue, everything influences the brain."

I was utterly shocked. There was no way I could be telling myself these things. I had no control at all. The way the voice was communicating to me was beyond where I was. However, I continued to listen. I opened my eyes for a moment as I lay on my back on the bed. To my left and right were lamps that were dimmed. When I closed my eyes, I could feel two people standing to my right and left. I opened my eyes again only to see the lamps. When I closed my eyes again, I was suddenly somewhere else. This time, I was lying on a metal table in what seemed to be a spaceship. I only figured so because I looked up briefly to look around the new space I was in and could see windows with the view of a vast black sky filled with stars. Two my right and left were two humanoid beings. They were wearing white and grey one-piece suits. Their heads were somewhat large, with large eyes and small mouths, like your typical grey alien, but they were much more human-like with beige/pink skin. The being on the left was typing on a holographic tablet screen, while the being on the right was solely focused on me. I heard a soft voice from within me say, "It's all right, you are safe. We are just monitoring you; everything is fine. You are safe." I opened my eyes again and gasped. I hoped that the journey was over, but could still feel the spirit molecule pull me in one last time.

The voice from the beginning came back. This time, I was in the dark blankness of my mind. Now with a different message.

"Stop doing all the different drugs. You don't need them. Let me demonstrate." I heard what sounded like a snap of a finger, and suddenly, I felt like I was at the peak of an LSD trip, then another snap, now at the peak of an MDMA trip, and then suddenly back.

"See. It's all within you. You don't even need DMT. So, stop it all now." I could feel that the voice was beginning to leave. But now I had the sense in me to speak up, "Wait. Who are you? Where are you?"

"You cannot and will not ever see me. I am beyond your reality. I am so far beyond you, it may be perceived as if I am millions of light-years away. But that is still not accurate." At that moment, I got but a mere glimpse at where the voice was coming from. The being seemed gargantuan and dark. It looked like a black pit of nothingness that stretched on forever.

I slowly began to sit up. I rubbed my eyes and face and laughed. It felt like I was gone for hours. When I asked my friends, they said it was no more than ten minutes! My throat still felt raw and burnt from the smoke, my brain felt a bit heavy, yet I felt good overall. It took some time to feel like myself again, no more than two hours. I recalled the entire experience like I normally do after a psychedelic, but it was different this time. I recalled how intimate the communication was. It was as though that being knew me very well, so much so that it felt like it knew more about me than I do! The warning about not doing psychedelics was worrisome to me since they were a significant part of my life at that time. Though I can remember the experience quite vividly, I always come back to that moment. I figured that with all internal spiritual guidance, true benevolent beings do not have an absolute stance. I remember Krishna and how serene, peaceful, and powerful its presence was. And I specifically remember that there wasn't any communication or guidance, no suggestion or ideological illumination within that presence. It was just pure presence, celebration, and joy. If I can take anything from that experience as something that is truly genuine, it was Krishna's presence. I saw that the golden light came from within me. It wasn't a being far away somewhere hiding and telling me what's best for me. Krishna came in a brilliance of golden light, ushering its presence within beautiful colors, sounds, aromas, and visuals. As potent as the second stage of my journey was, I find much more significance in the synchronicity of Krishna. Krishna came to me in a dream, I stumbled upon Krishna's celebration in the streets of Calgary, and I summoned Krishna from the depths of my being to directly be in its presence.

The Great Spirit of Crescent Falls

"Doug is dead." These are three words I thought I would never hear, three words that filled me with so much confusion, sadness, anger, and turmoil. I received that phone call from a friend around 1 p.m. Almost immediately, my mind was filled with memories of our childhood together. Doug and I had first met at Elmwood Elementary School when we were seven years old. Though he had been in and out of my life throughout my teen years, we found each other again in our early twenties. We lived dramatically different lives.

Nonetheless, our friendship was just as it was from the beginning, full of jokes, laughter, and good times. He was on the rebound from a life of crime and darkness. He began to confide in Kris and I, promising that he could change and relinquish his past life of drugs and violence. It honestly looked very promising. I remember when I went to visit him in Vancouver when I was twenty-one. He had been staying with his girlfriend at the time, just until he returned to Edmonton to straighten out his life. She significantly influenced him to change his ways. Our visit was the beginning of our rekindled friendship, and it felt so good to know that he was looking forward to getting back to regular "honest" work. A strange moment occurred that scared me while we were walking to a McDonald's in downtown Vancouver. "He's going to die in two years." The voice was a sharp whisper in the darkness of my mind. It came out of nowhere. I didn't know what the think, what to say; I just looked at him and said to myself, *No way.*

No less than a year later, Doug had moved into the same apartment complex as me. It was great having him so close. Though he was still struggling with his criminal lifestyle, he was trying to spend more time with Kris and I. We spoke to him about all kinds of new age subjects and philosophies that we were learning at the time. I had completely forgotten about that voice. I truly thought I was making a great impact. I would ask him what it would take for him to become clean and begin the process of letting go of his addictions. The trust was there, and I knew it would take some time.

Another year had gone and by, and I had made several different moves from the apartment complex, to my parents' house, and into a studio apartment downtown. I began my first year at Grant MacEwan University as a psychology major. By this time, Doug and I went our separate ways again. I would hear from him now and again, which was nice, and the last time I heard from him was a phone call from a camp he was working at. He shared with me that he planned to propose to his girlfriend and that he was working to make enough money to pay off some debt and then move to Vancouver to start a new life with her. *He did it,* I thought to myself. It was great to hear. After two years of watching him turn his life around, it was amazing to know that he was now on the right path.

It was May 15, 2011, when I got the call. Doug had died in his sleep of heart failure. Throughout his life, he had underlining health conditions that he never took too seriously. I remember when we were in the second grade, the first year we met. We were playing in the park, and he was standing on the very top of the big red slide. It was around fifteen feet high. There were several kids around the mouth of the slide, and in the blink of an eye, one kid was pushed into another, and Doug fell. He hit his head on the concrete curb eight feet from the slide that bordered the sand. An ambulance was called, and he was swiftly taken to the hospital. We were so young and didn't know what to think; everyone was in shock. Since that moment, he has suffered from spells of epilepsy. I thought he could have developed a heart condition from the brain damage he received from the fall so many years ago, but I just didn't know. I thought it could have been his drug use, but I didn't understand how MDMA or cocaine could cause heart failure in someone while they were asleep. I just didn't know.

That night, I couldn't hold it in anymore. I burst into tears and cried until I fell asleep. My childhood friend Kris, Teela, a friend I met at university, and I decided to spend the next weekend at Crescent Falls. It's a beautiful double waterfall near Nordegg, Alberta. It was Doug's funeral that Friday as well, but I didn't have it in me to go. At the time, I couldn't muster up the strength to be around all our old childhood friends—people I hadn't seen for many years, people I had lost touch with, people I couldn't trust anymore. Instead, I planned to have my own little ceremony at Crescent Falls. I packed a few things for the weekend, including several crystals, and we made our way to the falls.

The first day we hiked around the falls to take in the fresh mountain air, make our camp, and settle in. The next day, we hiked down to the basin of the first waterfall. While Kris and Teela were taking in the sun and the mist and power of the waterfall, I decided to hike down to the second waterfall where the river continues off into the thick forest of coniferous trees. I planned to make a shrine for Doug. I found a spot where the river pooled off to the side for a perfect little beach. I took out the crystals that I packed and made a shrine to honor Doug in the only way I knew how. After constructing the shrine, I sat silently with my eyes closed.

I began remembering random times from our childhood: listening to music in his bedroom, feeding his pet turtle, walking around neighborhoods, smoking weed, and him telling me, "Stop being so paranoid, no one cares, besides no one is even around," and it dawned on me that we never argued, never gotten into a fight, ever! All my memories of Doug are so happy, with so much laughter. I smiled and began to laugh. I started telling Doug about all the good memories I have of him and how good he was to me. I sat there for a few moments silently when I suddenly heard within me, *"I'm listening."* It was Doug's voice! It was so clear. It was also different. It was calm with a tone of relief. I opened my eyes and looked down at the shrine. A slight breeze picked up, and a leaf wiggled underneath one of the crystals. I didn't even notice that the leaf was there. I picked up the leaf, and I could feel Doug was with me. I put the leaf in the river. The leaf began to somehow make its way right toward the waterfall. I spoke openly to Doug, "No, man, that's not the life you want to go back to! Go with the river and into a life of ease and peace." Suddenly, the leaf turned around and made its way gently down the river to the left, where the river curved into the forest. Doug was gone. I smiled and truly felt that Doug was finally at peace.

Two months after Doug's death, I had a strange and wonderful dream. It began like a scene in *The Matrix.* I was in an underground parking lot, walking up to a door slightly cracked open. I could hear music thumping and colorful lights and lasers flashing through the threshold of the door. I opened the door and entered a nightclub full of people. The whole room was crowded, full of people dancing and enjoying themselves. I had a reserve within myself that wouldn't allow me to join the party. I glanced around the club, intuitively looking for something but not knowing exactly what. Off to my right, about one hundred meters away, I saw people going through another door. I instinctually followed the stream of people through the door. I was suddenly in a very large hallway. It was massive. The width was at least fifty feet, and the height of the ceiling just as high or more. The floor was slightly ramped upwards that led to an opening far ahead of me. I could see people all around me walking toward the gaping opening at the far end. At first, the opening was a wall of white light, but as I continued toward it, closer and closer, the light unveiled the other side. A vast meadow appeared with a clear open blue sky and a valley of trees and mountains off in the distance. The strange thing was that when I stepped through this new threshold into the meadow, I was suddenly in a large room with brick walls. There was a small section of floor that I was standing on that terminated in front of me into a pit of never-ending blackness. Scattered symmetrically and evenly in squares were platforms that floated in the blackness on even ground with the platform that I was on. Far ahead of me was another door. I knew that was the end. That was the door I was intuitively looking for. I knew I had to jump on each platform one at a time to make my way across to the platform the door was on. I jumped, made it to one, then another, and another, until the next one fell, and I plummeted into the black void. I didn't wake up, I didn't die, I was in the underground parking lot again. As if I was on autopilot, I made my way through the dream all over again. I found myself in the black void room again. I paused for a moment and thought to myself, *OK, one of the platforms is going to fall, but I don't know if they are random or if the same one will fall again.* I replayed the dream repeatedly. The platforms that fell were random, and over time, I was getting increasingly more frustrated. I got to the black void room once again. This time, I realized something. I've done this so many times that there had to be a time where I would make it. I suddenly got a brilliant idea. I stood on the platform, and I replayed all the times I started jumping on the platforms. All these versions of myself were jumping from platform to platform, and I stood there watching until I saw it! I saw the version where I was one platform away from the door. I transported myself into that version and made the final jump! I made it. I opened the door and walked through.

The dream shifted suddenly from the bottomless pit room to myself seated on a bamboo grass hut floor. Before I saw anyone, I heard a familiar voice, "Zoran! I'm here! I'm in Thailand. This is where I went. I always wanted to live here." Doug and his cousin Mitchel were suddenly sitting with me on the floor! I looked at Doug and smiled. Of course, this is where you'd go. A year later, I went to Thailand for the first time to attend a yoga school called Agama Yoga. I truly felt that Doug, that dream, and the synchronicities of meeting two Agama Yoga students in Edmonton led me to Thailand and the magic I experienced there.

Crescent Falls has always been a special place to me. I hold it dear in my heart. Several years later, my dear soul mate Alicia and I went to Crescent Falls for a weekend getaway with a clear intention to experience DMT together in nature. I told her the story of Doug and my experience with his spirit at the river. A refreshing feeling of happiness had arisen, thinking of Doug and being back at Crescent Falls. Alicia and I made our way down to the lower river to view the beauty of the double falls. My first thought was to find the shrine I had made for Doug. Of course, it was nowhere to be found. Six years had passed, so it made sense that the crystals had been washed away.

Nonetheless, I stood in the same spot, looking up at the waterfalls and thinking about Doug and how he influenced my life even after his death. I believe that the dream I had with Doug and finding him in Thailand sparked a momentum that inspired my travels to Thailand and India for yoga. Little did I know how Crescent Falls would add to the synchronicity.

We arrived at Crescent Falls on a Friday and decided that Saturday would be the day we would experience DMT. I woke up on Saturday morning feeling refreshed and nervous. DMT is a powerful substance, and even though I'm always left with a great feeling of warmth and compassion, I always feel anxiety leading up to the experience because of its immediate intensity. I shook off the nervous feelings as best as possible and found a spot next to the river to practice yoga and meditate.

The sun was climbing in the sky and warming the little spot of sand I was meditating on next to the river. The yoga practice and meditation spiraled into a depth of awareness and presence, sensitive to all the wildlife around me. I found myself naturally returning to my body, filling my lungs with the moist river air. I gently opened my eyes to allow the sunlight to stream in steadily when a strange sight caught my attention from the periphery of my left eye. I saw a woman dressed in a white gown with black hair cut just above her shoulders and bangs right above her eyes. I quickly looked to my left to see the woman when a glimmer of light trailed across the leaves of the bushes on the hill that ran along the river shore. I turned to face forward again and closed my eyes. *I definitely saw a woman there. I saw her.* I placed an image in my mind to recapture what she looked like as clearly as possible. I decided then not to tell Alicia. I felt a gentle guidance to trust what I saw and that synchronicity was at play.

I slowly made my way back up to our campsite to have breakfast and begin our journey of finding the perfect spot for our DMT experience. I confidently stated to Alicia that I had the perfect spot in mind. It was a mossy patch surrounded by trees with an opening to admire the majesty of the mountains. We went up to the river as it slowly dried up, leaving a wide track of rocks and pebbles. The river had receded under the rocks to emerge again into the waterfall behind us. We stumbled upon one mossy patch, but it was a little too close to our camp. A family was too close, and we just didn't feel comfortable knowing that someone could see us or smell the DMT, especially children. So, we continued forward. I noticed what kind of trees were around the first mossy patch we found and kept them in mind. I had a good feeling that if I were to see those same trees, we would find another mossy patch. After fifteen minutes of hiking, I noticed a similar grouping of trees up and to the left. The riverbank began to slope into a ledge with dark soil, and the trees became denser. I pointed at a spot a little higher up the ledge and said to Alicia that it would be the spot. We climbed the ledge and found a mossy patch surrounded by coniferous trees with a perfect opening that showcased the mountains in all their glory.

We laid a blanket down on the moss and brought out our makeshift DMT device. Alicia wanted to go first, so I packed up the device and started to burn the DMT until it was filled with smoke. Alicia inhaled and held her breath. After about thirty seconds, she exhaled and laid down. After ten minutes, Alicia slowly sat up and took a full deep breath. I wish I could share with you what her experience was. At the time, she didn't know how to explain what she experienced. She felt that it was best she kept it to herself and continue to feel the remnants of the fleeting DMT that was now starting to leave her.

It was my turn to go. I was facing the opening with the view of the mountains. Alicia lit the DMT for the device to fill with smoke. I took it to my lips and inhaled, filling my lungs with the hot, harsh, and bitter smoke. I held my breath, and no more than ten seconds had gone by when the forest and mountains started to twist and spiral in fractal patterns. I smiled and exhaled the stale smoke and laid back onto the blanket and moss with my eyes closed. I could feel the ground all around me. The Earth's presence was a warm welcome as the sun peeked through the tops of trees up above and shined single rays upon me. The warmth was dancing with bliss when I heard a voice. "Doesn't this feel so good? Isn't it amazing to feel the bugs crawling in the soil? To feel the trees' roots dig deep, and the branches to rise high for the wind to caress them? This is what I feel at all times." I felt myself sink deeper and deeper into the ground, surrounded by the Earth's warm embrace and love.

The DMT gently drifted away, and I returned to my body from what felt like hours bathing in the soil beneath me. However, as always, only ten or so minutes had gone by. I sat up and looked at Alicia. She had a peculiar look in her eyes like she had been startled by something. I began to tell her about my experience, and when I finished, she said, "I have to tell you something. When you were about to lay down, from the corner of my eye, I saw a woman kneel down and go into your body."

I could feel the color drain from my face. "Did she have a long white gown on, and was her hair black and less than shoulder length?" I asked.

"Yes! Wait, how did you know that?" Alicia asked with a bewildered curiosity. I explained to her my vision after my meditation, and we were both left, in all honesty, feeling weirded out. However, we decided that the woman was beneficent as she had shown herself to both of us in a friendly way. After some time, absorbing all the magic of the little green paradise we were in, it was time to head back to camp for lunch and continue with our day.

The woman in the white dress had made a significant imprint within me. The experience of deeply feeling the Earth and being guided so lovingly into the bliss of her abode was an initiation. I've come to add her to my prayers when I practice yoga and meditation. However, the woman in the white dress isn't truly a suiting name. When I recall my experience with her, she felt so much more than just a woman. She is a great spirit who resides at Crescent Falls, guiding anyone sensitive enough into her abode of love and earthly bliss. Thus, I thought it was suiting to call her The Great Spirit of Crescent Falls. Alicia and I stayed for a final night under the starry night with the rushing river soothing us to sleep. Our weekend getaway to Crescent Falls was more adventurous than we could have imagined. We swam in the waterfalls, climbed rocky hills into forests with great boulders covered in moss looking like sentinels from an ancient forgotten world, and marveled at crystal clear night skies, unveiling constellations seldom seen in a city. The Great Spirit danced within my mind as I remembered curiously of the shimmering light across the leaves as we drove back home, back to our regular life.

The Great Spirit of Crescent Falls has stayed well within my heart ever since that fateful day. I enjoy finishing my yoga practice and meditation with a grateful prayer to my masters and herself, giving thanks for her presence and love, and for her role in deepening the connection that Alicia and I still have to this day. Little did I know that soon enough, another great spirit would enter my life.

The Journey to Ayahuasca

There has been one challenging reoccurring lesson in my life that has demanded patience repeatedly. This lesson has ranged from small ordinary occasions to large significant life events. It seems that we are all born into this world already equipped with repeating lessons, begging for the right kind of attention that will finally end the cycle of suffering that is inherent within the lesson. Because we are all unique, yes all 7.6 billion of us, there's no way to know your reoccurring lesson. I'm not one to try to convince anyone that I am at all powerful enough, psychic enough, or enlightened enough to read your soul and affirm that your lesson is exactly what I think. What I can do is share with you what my lesson is, how I came to figure it out, and how I deal with the reoccurring cycles because, in all honesty, the lesson is still very much present in my life. I have learned deeply that these lessons aren't meant to be abolished. They are the very fabric of our human condition and will remain intact just as our skin will remain on our bones until we die. Though we may suffer by not accepting how intimate the lesson is and how integrated it is within our very being, it is possible to develop a keen, deliberate vision that perceives the lesson, clearly leading to *the* decision that prevents suffering and promotes self-mastery.

My life lesson is this; I invite myself into people's lives, projects, events, or anything that I feel like I would benefit from, and it almost always backfires. Throughout my adolescence, I navigated through many confusing emotional moments of lacking understanding that anytime and anywhere I inserted myself, I would inevitably be ridiculed, undermined, or completely ignored. When I was a child, this lesson was very difficult because I was stubborn. However, in my mind, I didn't perceive myself as being stubborn but more so curious and adamant that I *should be* invited and accepted. Every time the lesson would play out and inevitably end in loneliness, rather than looking at myself and considering whether it was something I was doing, I would lash out and place blame and anger on the "friends" who were being mean or didn't care about me. However, the fact was that I was putting myself into situations where I didn't belong or fit in. It took being around people who chastised and humiliated me to initiate the lesson that harmony in my life comes from being invited. I didn't fully realize this until one fateful day.

In December 2010, Kris and I entered a local metaphysical store called Creation of a New Dawn for the first time on a whim to begin our collection of crystals and new age books. I was in awe of all the new age materials, crystals, tarot decks, and other mystical objects that were all so new to me. A woman emerged from a small room at the back of the store and introduced herself, "Hi there, I'm Dawn, welcome to my store and Merry Christmas!" As she approached to greet us, she looked at me with a sudden change of expression and intensity. Dawn began to speak directly to me about my life, father, and, most importantly, South America. "You will go to South America. You must. But you will need to be invited because you have some dark karma that needs to be healed before you can enter." I didn't know what to say. It was all a bit too much. At that time, I was so new to the whole idea of channeling and readings. She immediately apologized and said, "I'm a little drunk right now. It's Christmas, so I've had a couple of drinks. When I drink, I begin to channel, and it's hard to stop sometimes!" We laughed together, and she looked at me again and asked me a startling question, "You're going somewhere over Christmas? You shouldn't go." I was, indeed, going somewhere. I was going to Vancouver to stay with a young woman named Brenna I met over the summer. Dawn had picked up on my life lesson. I was inviting myself into Brenna's life, and I was too ignorant to understand that what I was doing wasn't going to end so happily ever after. Though I ignored Dawn's advice about Vancouver because of my stubborn ego and all the plans I had with Brenna, her words about South America stuck within my mind and heart.

Dawn was the first person in my life to directly tell me that I shouldn't invite myself to places and into people's lives. Though I'm now good friends with Brenna, it became clear after my time in Vancouver that our connection wasn't meant to be more than friendship. The more I reflected on Dawn's words and the possibility of eventually traveling to South America, the more I observed how often I invite myself into people's lives. It dawned on me that the reason I would go to South America would be for a life-changing experience with ayahuasca. The problem at that time was that I didn't know anyone in South America, I didn't know anyone going

114

to South America, and I didn't know anyone who regularly journeyed with ayahuasca.

The idea of going to South America sat in the back of my mind. On random occasions, I would think about trying to go to South America, but the thought alone scared me. To be in the Amazon Jungle with people who only spoke Spanish or Portuguese, navigating a completely foreign terrain was out of my scope of possibility. I continued my life as it was in Edmonton, a university student beginning the practice of yoga and learning all I could about consciousness. Traveling alone was something I managed to do when it came to Canada and the US. By 2012, I had completed several trips to Vancouver and New York, and my confidence was growing. I was following an unknown synchronicity of development that led to my first international travel to Thailand. It seemed that the more I deepened my yoga practice, the synchronicity grew alongside it. I knew that South America was the goal ultimately, and to journey into the heart of the Amazon, I needed that invite.

When I attended the Akhanda Yoga TTC in 2016, all my patience had finally proven its worth. My ashram roommate Samarpan Anand invited me to Brazil to meet a family he had stayed with many times and to attend a yoga retreat called Vishva Shanti Retreats. During that training, he official birthed the idea and formulated what the entire eight-day retreat would entail. I was inundated in the best way possible with many stories from Samarpan about a family that lives in the middle of the Amazon in northern Brazil and their tree climbing, eco-tourism company Amazon Emotions. Every story settled deeper and deeper into my heart, and I knew without a shadow of a doubt that I would venture into the Amazon with him. For the next three years after the training, Samarpan, a few others, and I planned the first Vishva Shanti retreat in the summer of 2019.

During the winter of 2018, Alicia and I finally decided that we couldn't go to the retreat. The winters in Edmonton are harsh. At the time, my work consisted of seasonal contracts and renovation work, and our finances couldn't support paying for our livelihood and the necessary cost of the retreat. The idea of coming up with thousands of dollars in a few months was stressful. However, one phone call with Samarpan changed everything. He is an incredibly motivating person. With his help, I put into perspective everything Alicia and I could do to raise all the funds for the retreat. It was that month Alicia launched her apothecary business, *Wild Bloom Botanicals*. With her newly created herbal products, my private yoga classes, oracle readings, and guitar lessons, we raised all the money we needed over five months to make it to Brazil! We received so much support from our friends and family that we made enough to buy both of our return flights in the first two weeks of fundraising. It certainly was a miracle! The synchronicity was growing with every passing day. We were harmonizing with the mystical rhythm, and life was showing its great blossoms of love and wonder.

Stop. Take three deep breaths. So far, you have been reading so much about my life. I promise you that it is building up to a great discovery. There is still some way to go, so please be patient! There is a great treasure and gift at the end of this road.

Samarpan spoke highly of the family in Brazil. Their love and wisdom seemed to transverse space and time and pour out of Samarpan as he shared many stories of their lives. Vanessa and Leo are the creators of Amazon Emotions and have built a wonderful retreat center in the middle of a vast valley in the Amazon Jungle. They have six hundred acres of jungle that they protect through an initiative called The Jaguar Project, where they have trail cameras that track the jaguars' movement throughout the jungle. The eco-tourism side of their business is based on ascending three mighty trees they call the Princess, Queen, and King. The part of their home that captured my heart is their beautiful jungle garden. Leo has spent the better part of a decade learning everything he can to transform the secondary growth of harsh spiny, defensive jungle into a lush, abundant garden full of bananas, papayas, ginger, turmeric, passion fruit, oranges, moringa, and so much more!

The retreat was more than life-changing. The group was small and consisted of Megan, Doug, Brynne, Max, and Cristian who are all good friends with Samarpan, which made for an intimate week of daily yoga, jungle adventures, waterfalls, and tree climbing. Each day of the retreat was themed around a chakra; Day 1, Muladhara (root), Day 2 Svadhisthana (sacral), Day 3 Manipura (solar), Day 4 Anahata (heart), Day 5 Vishuddha (throat), Day 6 Ajna (third eye), and Day 7 Sahasrara (crown). Samarpan planned a full day adventure for each day that aligned with the chakra of the day. We started the day with a sunrise yoga class followed by breakfast, a philosophical discussion based on writing prompts, lunch, and then an afternoon adventure into the jungle on day 1, to a waterfall on day 2, an overnight trek deep into the jungle on day 3, and tree climbing on days 3 and 4. The day some of us went to climb the Princess will forever be etched in my heart. It was the day I proposed to my dear soul mate Alicia.

We had spoken about marriage and children many times leading up to the retreat, and I thought that if I were to propose, what better place than in the middle of paradise. It was June 28, and Alicia and I were accompanied by Leo, Samarpan, Megan, Brynne, Doug, and Cristian. I was secretly very nervous. Everyone knew about the proposal except Alicia, of course. Though my nervous mind was hidden underneath my brimmed blue hat, I couldn't help but think about all the things I would say to Alicia once we were safely in the treetop canopy, high above the other trees. The ascent seemed to take a lifetime. I worried something would go wrong with the ropes and that we would plummet to our demise. What a thing to consider! The day our lives would change and begin the commitment of a married life together ended by no fault but our own!

While we all arrived safely in the branches of the Princess, Leo and Samarpan set up a hammock between two branches. Alicia and I struggled our way into comfortable positions to finally relax after about thirty minutes of slowly ascending to the tree top. Brynne began to sing a song we planned the day before. Her lovely voice carried all around us, serenading the surrounding jungle. I took Alicia's hands in mine and looked in her eyes. I could tell she was curious about the whole situation. I said with loving words, "Alicia, I love you so much, and I want us to live our lives together." I reached into my pocket for the little box the ring was nestled in. I pulled out the ring and asked her *the question,* "Alicia, will you marry me?" She did indeed say yes! We kissed, and the others cheered and clapped to love that was bonded even deeper while embraced by the mighty and beautiful Princess. We remained in the treetop to watch the sunset, and then made our way back down to solid ground.

During the retreat, we all made such a wonderful, deep soul connection with each other. One night, Vanessa told us that she loved our group and that watching us all fall in love with the jungle was a special sight. She has seen so many groups of people come and go, but our group stood out as one that she would remember fondly. It was the first yoga retreat that they hosted on their property, and it surely will not be the last.

One by one, Alicia and I said goodbye to our new friends. We had several days left until our flight home, so we decided to stay and prepare for a new journey: ayahuasca. We spoke with Leo about taking ayahuasca the day after everyone left, but for whatever reason, the day was delayed, again and again. Our day of departure back to Manaus was approaching quickly. We realized that our time with ayahuasca wasn't meant to be. Other guests would arrive spontaneously, and there was a group of high school students from all over the US that were there as well. Alicia and I both intuited that forcing the experience didn't feel right, so we surrendered and finally decided it wasn't our time yet. The day had come for us to leave the jungle paradise and make our way back home.

It was just shortly after 7 p.m., Samarpan and I were sitting on the veranda talking about all we had done to prepare for what was to come next. We sat in the twilight of the sky as the last rays of the sun were slowly diminishing, and the first stars started to speckle the looming blackened sky. A full year had gone by since Alicia and I had taken on the challenge of raising funds for the first retreat. Now, Samarpan and I were back in the jungle patiently waiting for the ayahuasca to kick in.

Throughout the summer, Samarpan and I prepared for an international travel expo we were invited to in October. It was a huge step for us as new business partners and the budding Vishva Shanti Retreat. Samarpan came up to Edmonton from California where he lived and studied at the Palmer University to become a chiropractor. While he stayed with Alicia and I, we discussed going back to Brazil in the winter to plan the next retreat. The desire to do ayahuasca had been in the back of my mind ever since the retreat, and the opportunity had finally come. But when Samarpan and I spoke about it, I wasn't sure it would happen. I wanted it to be organic and something that aligned with what Dawn had said to me years ago.

The travel expo was a huge success! We partnered with a local rock climbing business called Vertically Inclined to set up a tree climbing experience where ropes were hung from the rafters of the building so that people could get an idea of what it would be like to climb a one hundred and fifty-foot tree in the jungle. We had groups of people around our booth constantly for the two days of the expo, and two people climbing all day periodically. It was exhilarating to have that much attention. We felt like our purpose was clear, and the Universe was supporting our efforts. After the weekend, we left the expo feeling great about our efforts to get a new group of ten people on the next retreat.

Samarpan spent another day with us, and we discussed our next travel to Brazil. The intention was rooted in spending time with Vanessa and Leo and having clear conversations about the future of Vishva Shanti. There is a deep need in the Amazon to support the Indigenous tribes. Our mission was to be of service not only to the people who come on the retreat but also to the inhabitants of the home we have come to love. However, ayahuasca was calling as well. Though soft and seemingly gentle, we both recognized that the time for us may have come.

The sun had fully set. Samarpan and I expressed how important we are to each other. We are the *brajanandas*, how could our teacher Vishvji have known? In the span of three years, we were roommates at an ashram, sharing our life stories with each other to sitting on a wooden platform overlooking the jungle and about to have a completely life-changing experience. Everything we had done in our lives had led up to that moment. The Universe had conspired for this meeting beyond what we could have comprehended. I stopped going to university, and Samarpan delayed his entrance into chiropractic school to go to India. The mystical rhythm of life had harmonized to create a convergence of two souls destined to make a great impact in the world.

After forty minutes of talking and meditating, the ayahuasca began to show herself. The initial feeling was a soft joyfulness that grew into slight tingling in my hands, through my arms, and up my spine. My vision began to slightly swirl as the potency rose, signaling to lay down in the hammock waiting for me. As I arose, the ayahuasca began to swell and churn. With each step, the DMT twisted the very fabric of my mind into spirals of colors, and pulsations of sensation pushed me closer toward the hammock. A silent voice was emerging like an aum of a thousand Tibetan monks sounding off in the immediate distance. As soon as I laid down in the hammock, the intense geometric internal visuals began. It started very similarly to when I smoked DMT. However, I even had a thought that there was a very noticeable difference. The voice was ever-present and seemingly invasive. *This is similar to DMT, I can handle this,* I thought, and the voice responded. *"It has only begun."* Right at that moment, great intensity of sensation, beyond anything I could ever imagine, had gripped me totally. The hallucinations were alive. Mother Ayahuasca had arrived. I was totally gripped by her presence, control, and guidance. It was as though I was strongly held in place by a pair of hands that belonged to a giant as the ayahuasca coursed through my veins. The rainbow, metallic, geometric shapes organized themselves, and I was face to face with the Sri Yantra. It was simultaneously far away from me and cascading right into me and all around me. The stacking triangles that formed around me three-dimensionally held within them a wild array of geometric shapes and coalescing images and faces. When I looked away from the Sri Yantra, and into the geometries the triangles were making, full physical images would appear and disappear. It was very hard to hold my gaze at any one spot for too long. The physical sensations of the ayahuasca were extreme. Imagine that your senses have a dial. Right now, that dial is on low. When we experience anxiety, the dial turns up somewhat, and when we have a panic attack, it seems like the dial has been cranked halfway. When we experience depression, it's like the dial has been turned down even lower than the farthest point to the left. It almost seems impossible for the dial to go any lower. Ayahuasca has complete control of the dial. In the beginning, the dial is cranked to the fullest and then removed. There is no option than to be with all your senses completely heightened to the point of terror and death. It is beyond immense. The feeling of dread within this whirlwind of psychedelia shared an absolute wonderment that the Sri Yantra was right there in all its glory without my conscious will of imagining it, without my prior desire to see it, and with a life of its own, calling to me into its center where great peace, joy, and bliss reside. But I couldn't do it. I couldn't go into the portal. I've done it so many times in the past. The intensity of what was happening physically was pulling me away, and I couldn't stop it. The initial wave that grew seemed to grow perpetually without end. I didn't want to be in the ayahuasca's grip anymore, but the more I resisted it, the stronger it got. I peered into the Sri Yantra and felt a moment of safety in its presence. Through all the internal chaos and movement, I began to chant the heart mantra *Jaag Anahata Anandoham*. In response, the chaos laughed at me, and I heard the voice say, *"That will not work here! When you are sober, sure it will work, but you are in my realm now!"* I felt even more powerless, so I finally surrendered. I let it take over me, and at that moment, the urge to vomit come over me. At first, I tried with all my might to kept it down. There was no use; the grip that the ayahuasca had on me seemed to take hold of my stomach and push whatever was in it up and out. I immediately jumped out of my hammock and over to the edge of the veranda to vomit. Because I had eaten very little that day, I was dry heaving. Suddenly, something came. The ayahuasca that was in my stomach emerged and coated my esophagus, throat, and sinus on the way up. Only a small amount of matter left my body. I could taste the ayahuasca again and could feel it soaking into the tissues of my throat, sinus, spine, and brain. All the while, I could hear the voice tell me, *"Just watch,"* as my entire esophagus from the top of my throat all the way down to my stomach completely opened involuntarily, as two large chunks were pumped out of my stomach and my mouth. I let out a primordial roar into the jungle. Miraculously and precisely at that moment of release, the wave of psychedelia and chaos subsided, and I returned to a sober state momentarily. I slowly got up and returned to my hammock. I thought to myself that it must be over, but, of course, it was far from over. The voice said, *"I'm not done with you yet. Prepare, there is yet another one."* Unlike the first wave, which came on suddenly, the second wave crashed with force twice as powerful.

Throughout the second wave, it felt like my nervous system was on fire. There was a steady static of rapid and constant pulsations all throughout my body, particularly under my skin. Internally, the Sri Yantra was still strongly present; however, I couldn't keep my eyes closed for more than twenty seconds or so. The gyrating and flashing images, colors, and geometries taunted me at every moment when I tried to focus in on the Sri Yantra. I was jolted up and out of the hammock again. I quickly made my way to the end of veranda to purge once more. This time, nothing came out.

I touched my face with my hands as they shook from the nervousness. I said out loud, "I can't handle this. It's so intense." Talking out loud was strangely comforting, and a sense of ease subtly washed over me. All the while, I continued to hear the soft voice say, *"Just watch,"* and that I did.

Though my whole experience in this second wave was extremely turbulent, there was a serene sense of strength guiding me to learn from every part of the experience. The burning sensation was tormenting me to the brink of insanity, yet the voice kept me grounded. Amidst everything, I managed to look at what was behind all the psychedelia. A deep, expansive darkness reached down into a void. That is where the turbulence was coming from. That is where the urges to jump up, scream, and run into the jungle was coming from. In that instance, a face flashed before me. It was strangely familiar. The face had two large wide-open eyes and a big open mouth with four fangs, two on top that curved outwards to the left and right, and two on the bottom that also curved outwards to the left and right. Its skin was green and yellow with red lips, white teeth, and white eyes. The Sri Yantra appeared in the center of its forehead and then ascended far ahead of me into a point, cascading its geometries down toward me through the face.

As the face disappeared, the second wave ended. The voice began to explain what had happened to my nervous system. *"Do not be afraid. You have not been harmed, though it may have felt painful. What you felt was me integrating into your nervous system. Your body couldn't fully digest the liquid; it had to be brought up and absorbed into your spine. I am now forever a part of you. Call upon me whenever you like, and use me. I will not ever intrude in your life."* Hearing Mother Ayahuasca say that she is now forever a part of me concerned me at first. I didn't ask for that. I didn't even know I wanted that. After a short while, I felt more and more comfortable with the fact that she was with me. The burning sensation was now a warm fuzzy feeling. That feeling began to merge with the next wave, and now, the intensity turned into an immense feeling of love and compassion. Mother Ayahuasca hugged me and held me in her presence. The tight grip had eased off, and I no longer felt so disoriented. The chaotic psychedelic visuals started subsiding into soft flashes of my life. The waves were now shorter and less intense; however, each wave showed me patterns of my behaviors and personality. Each wave brought on a great feeling of love and happiness, followed by a deep processing of witnessing how beliefs I've been carrying around have been adopted, and patterns that I have perpetuated throughout my life. *Just watch, just watch, just watch,* became my mantra. I was shown how much my parents have influenced my behaviors. I saw many images and scenes of myself watching and listening to how my parents spoke to each other, how my dad would speak to me when I asked him challenging questions, and how I began to act as my parents without even knowing it. I was reassured that human life is a continual development of patterns. It is up to me at this moment to develop patterns that can help me now but can be undone later in my life when they no longer serve me. I was shown the patterns between my brother Adam and I. Ayahuasca sent a different guide in this situation. Instead of witnessing all the negative behaviors, I was guided to choose love. I saw a vision of Adam in front of me, and I said, "I love you. Thank you for everything you've done to support me. I'm here because of you and all you've done to accept my way of life." Finally, the ayahuasca showed me Alicia. A sharp pang pinched my lower back, where I've had pain for several months. Mother Ayahuasca spoke up and said, "*That pain is Alicia.*" I burst out in laughter! I laughed, and laughed. The laughter was relieving happiness. The realization sparked a joy in understanding how I've been facilitating emotional pain between us. The pain I was causing her was the pain she was causing me. I looked at the vision of Alicia and felt immense love and forgiveness. The pain will go away when I choose to soften in times of arguments and tension. The more I choose to soften and see her pain as my pain, the opportunity will come when the pain will release, and her pain of not fully being accepted will be released. I gazed upon the image of Alicia and softly said, "I love you so much, and I will do everything I can to be supportive and caring. Your love is my love." Far too often, we personalize emotions that our loved one expresses to us. Sometimes we cannot be so perfect in communicating what is troubling us, and sometimes it comes out as aggression and anger. When we can look through the heart and view our loved ones with compassion, the pain will not stick as a personal attack. In my case, I had placed our arguments in my lower back. Though Mother Ayahuasca had shown me the source of my back pain, it would still take me some time to fully heal from it, and learn how to realign my hips to allow the wound-up muscles in my lower back to unwind and release the stuck emotions. That is synchronicity. We try to remedy minor physical pain with pills and ointments when in truth, a realization needs to occur that the source of the pain is also emotional. Once that realization occurs, synchronicity arises to teach how to find the misalignment in the clearest way possible. It can be as simple as a hip that is slightly out that can be adjusted with proper posture, physical therapy, exercise, or help from a chiropractor. When there is a predominant focus on the psychological ailments of the pain, synchronicity to find the source is ignored, leading to a perpetuation of the stories and beliefs within the pain's memory.

With each dip between the waves, Mother Ayahuasca would speak to me about her story. Now, I must say, there is no way for me to absolutely corroborate what I've been told with any viable historical literature. I know that may be troubling; however, I recognize that within a profound personal experience of communication with an otherworldly entity that knowledge can be expounded that turns out to be closely relative to information another person is compiling, the stream of synchronicity and the mystical rhythm extend beyond the individual and throughout humanity. It may seem that the above paragraph contradicts itself. What is important is the vastness of human potential and ideation. Though what I am about to share may not be immediately accessible through conventional, mainstream outlets, there is always an underground and independent source that makes its way through society to offer a new view of history.

During the third stage of my experience with the ayahuasca, I managed to keep my eyes closed for extended periods of time. There was a moment I opened my eyes and looked over to Samarpan. He was lying on his back with the top of his head toward the jungle. I could see a beam of golden light stream from his head, into the jungle, and up into the sky. At that moment, I heard Mother Ayahuasca speak to me, *"Ayahuasca is very old. The form that you have taken tonight is a crude form of it. At one point, far into the past of your humanity, it was in a much more refined form. Much of your humanity at that time enjoyed their version of ayahuasca. At that time, the world was in a time of great peace and prosperity. The ayahuasca bridged the minds of your humanity, linking all together, sharing a deep love and compassion that the ayahuasca facilitated. Because of great catastrophes and societal collapses, the ayahuasca was brought to Indigenous people worldwide to preserve. The people were taught which plants could be brought together to create the original form of ayahuasca. It is my goal to help humanity spread ayahuasca so that it can return to its refined form."* The waves were becoming smaller and smaller, and the voice was quieter through each wave. Before she left, Mother Ayahuasca comforted me by saying, *"Everything will be good. You will return to yourself with me as a kind of superpower. Bring awareness to your nervous system that I am a part of, and add me to your focus. Be open, go beyond."*

Leo had been present for our journeys the entire time. His presence was a noticeable grounding force that helped me return to my connection with Mother Ayahuasca and her guides. The dark void that I mentioned earlier was not a safe place to enter. There were many times when I would hear a different voice beckon me into the void. I knew clearly that I was not ready to go there. At one point in the first wave, I remember I had a moment of clarity that if chanting yogic mantras wouldn't work, the Great Spirit of Crescent Falls could. I repeated to myself, "Remember the Earth, remember the Earth, remember the Earth." I realized then that the darkness was trying to take me away to be forgotten. It was a test. Though my journey from that point on continued to be turbulent, tormenting, and chaotic, Mother Ayahuasca and her guides stepped in through my chanting. My journey was for me, not for an outer journey into the cosmos or a wandering into a dark void. I needed cleansing and healing, for I have not yet found my torch of light to explore regions completely foreign to my consciousness. Though Leo wouldn't agree with me here, he is a guide of Mother Ayahuasca, a holder of light in the darkness. Leo isn't a shaman; he would say he is more so a simple servant and maker of ayahuasca, and an explorer of her realms.

Leo played music at certain times throughout the night. Some songs were icaros from shamans he was familiar with, and some were not, yet they were still powerful at combatting the dark void. He would play a song at the perfect moment. I would think that I would like for a song to play, and there it started! And there were times when I spoke out loud to Leo to play a song, and he wouldn't! I could only laugh at his silence while hearing Mother Ayahuasca say, *"Just watch,"* and realize that sometimes I need to face the chaos on my own.

The journey with ayahuasca must be opened and closed to contain the experience and protect our consciousness. Leo explained to us that the realm we enter with ayahuasca is the *borrachera*. Though *borrachera* translates to "drunkenness" in Spanish, Leo defined it as the "strange mystery" in the context of ayahuasca. The intention of opening and closing the journey is to keep the *borrachera* in the realm of ayahuasca. Leo shared with us stories of people who did not close the journey properly, and the *borrachera* continued in their daily life. When the journey began, Leo asked Samarpan and I three questions to open the experience. Leo asked, *"Como Vai* (How are you?), *Voce tem la borrachera?* (Do you have the strange mystery?), *and Voce tem luce?* (Do you have the light?). We were to respond to each question, good, yes, and yes. At the end of the journey, Leo intuitively knew when to ask us the questions and to close the journey. The important part is saying no to the second question. We must make it clear to the ayahuasca and to ourselves that the *borrachera* has ended.

I managed to get out of my hammock and feel a resemblance of my sober self, yet still very much subtly feeling the remnants of the ayahuasca. I made my way to the room Samarpan and I were sharing to lie down and rest from nearly five hours of a deep dive into the *borrachera*. Samarpan had a completely different experience than me. His was not turbulent at all. He didn't have to vomit, and the process of integrating the ayahuasca was smooth. After our journey, he shared with me that when I was vomiting, the ayahuasca said to him, *"You see? I could be like that with you, but I won't. He needs to purge and experience the chaos."*

I want you to know that I do not mean to scare you. Every ayahuasca journey is a very personal and intimate experience. I realized that deeply when Samarpan and I compared each other's intensities. I cannot suggest you seek out ayahuasca because it's not something I actively sought out. Ayahuasca came into my life through a series of interconnecting synchronicities, as you've read above. Please take into consideration that ayahuasca is a beautiful and powerful tool for self-discovery.

Samarpan made his way down to the main kitchen and living area to spend some time with the family. I simply did not have the energy to try at that moment. I laid in bed, restless, trying to get some sleep. The *borrachera* was still moving within me. I tried many times to command the *borrachera* to stop and that it was over. With little success, I got up and went down to the kitchen area. I wasn't down there long for the lights and sound of people talking was overwhelming. I managed to spend a few minutes drawing the face that appeared to me in the second wave. Taking the time to draw the face was soothing and therapeutic in a strange way.

Afterward, I walked up to our room and finally fell asleep. Throughout the night, I would suddenly wake up to the *borrachera* moving around within me. It seemed I was woken up every hour. When the sun finally started to rise, and daylight crept into the room, I laid on my back with my eyes closed. I gazed firmly at the *borrachera* within my mind and concentrated on it. I spoke loudly in my mind, *"NO, it is over. Leave now."* Like a wisp of smoke, the *borrachera* dissipated. The movement had settled, and a soft serenity washed over my body. That day and the next, I spent a lot of time with Leo in his separate jungle home and garden, away from the main house. Many insights began to blossom in my mind regarding all the wonders Mother Ayahuasca had shown me. I thought a lot about what she said to me near the end of my journey. I wasn't sure to believe that the Ayahuasca was a substance that an ancient advanced civilization had consumed and brought to the current Indigenous in South America. Leo expressed to Samarpan and me that even though there is a lot of truth dissemination, there are many illusions and distractions as well. The colorful array of visions and prophetic images are to be analyzed and scrutinized. If we fall victim to believing in everything we see, it can be an invitation for the *borrachera* to continue influencing daily decisions. There were many times during my journey that I was told to go off into the jungle. As convincing it may be that because of the power of ayahuasca, you'll be safe, it is advised to never go into the jungle alone, especially during the first time experiencing ayahuasca! Leo, who can be considered a veteran with hundreds of experiences with ayahuasca, has never gone into the jungle alone.

Periodically throughout the final days of our stay in paradise, I would bring attention to my nervous system and call upon Mother Ayahuasca. Like she said, I immediately felt the nerves in my arms and chest, leading right into my heart. The feelings would concentrate slightly and tingle as if I were building up energy through my heart and arms. The day after the journey, I held silence as much as I could. My time was spent drawing the face and other abstract drawings that could represent what I experienced. The phrase, "Be Open, Go Beyond" repeated naturally in my mind as I wrote it out in calligraphy over and over. With each repetition, doors within the memory of my ayahuasca journey unveiled bits of insight and wisdom about how to integrate the experience back into my daily life. The first insight was to relax and slow down while still being present with the people around me. There was a subtle urge to go into my hammock and stay there incapacitated. However, I knew that I needed interaction and enjoyment of laughing with Leo's children, expressing my visions through art, and breathing in the fresh jungle air. Secondly, time with Leo was healing. Being in the presence of someone who is largely unfettered by the capitalistic consuming world was refreshing and inspiring. His life is the jungle. Every day, he is experimenting with growing techniques to improve his garden's efficiency while surrendering to the uncontrollable factors of the jungle environment. For instance, Samarpan and I were on their property during the rainy season; however, it didn't rain once during the week we were there. The sky was clear blue with a scorching hot sun. It was unheard of at that time of year to have seven consecutive days of sun. What I learned was that at that exact time, the Earth's perihelion was occurring where the sun was its closest to the Earth in their orbit. Now, I know it's a stretch to suggest a correlation and causation when it can easily and more likely be attributed to climate change. Leo expressed that over the years, he has witnessed a gradual change in the rainy season. In the past, according to Leo, the rainy season started and stopped like clockwork. I feel that the interruptions of the ongoing rains are due to many reasons, the perihelion, climate change, mass deforestation, and polluting industries. At least that is what we typically hear of as causes. The more time I spent with Leo, the more I was inspired to live a simple life. He stressed to me how important our planet is and that the more we can live close to the Earth, the more we can help reverse the effects of climate change. That can mean being on your own land with personally built housing and growing most of your food. I imagined myself and Alicia, shifting our lifestyles to manifest such a dream, and here I was in the jungle with a man who was living it. I felt a blessing bestowed upon me most humbly through this elder of the jungle, giving me guidance on what it truly takes to live a self-sustainable life. The greatest keys to unlocking the door to the dream are patience, persistence, endurance, and the curiosity to learn from ancestral land stewardship methods. City dwellers have been deeply disconnected from the previous rural dwellers and their connections to the land. We think that the revolution will occur in the streets when the more impactful revolution is returning to the land.

The time had finally come for Samarpan and me to leave the jungle paradise and embark on our way back to our respective homes. The week seemed like a month, and a day at the same time. Each day was stretched by slow ease while packed with immense life lessons and life-altering synchronicities. I had gained a new perspective on who I am and how I can share my presence with the world. My invitation to the Amazon Jungle had been fulfilled more than I could imagine, and a great sense of responsibility had crystallized in my mind to seek a more natural life to truly help heal this planet.

You may be wondering, "How are these stories part of FLP?" Essentially, they trace the course of synchronicities delivered by my future self through the door in my heart. Each story navigates a series of events over the course of many years that interconnect my life experiences with the nonphysical realm of the heart. It's miraculous to think that the stories begin before the conception of FLP and my awareness of the heart's language, intuition, and intelligence. What FLP has done is allow me to perceive how to look for particular synchronicities that remind me of the feeling I recall from my experiences with Amareld and other versions of my future self. I am led to believe that we all operate this way; have momentary, seemingly random events that string together toward larger, more significant events. FLP has done wonders for me, and I have this very existence to thank. What seemed like small singular events have grown into a network of experiences that now feed into a great wealth of creativity and inspiration. With this knowledge, it is easy to foresee your path to actualize your harmonious future self. Thus, FLP is a means to bring awareness to the cycles of synchronicities that, in this part of the book, I have named the mystical rhythms and learn through continual meditation and learning precisely how the synchronicities manifest. There is yet a final stretch in this rabbit hole of synchronous mysteries.

CHAPTER 8

The Microdosing Body

T hank you, dear reader, for coming this far and taking the time to dive deep into the modality of FLP and following the journey into my phenomenal life stories. I understand that many of the stories I shared can be hard to believe. I ask you not to take my word for it, and instead search within yourself how phenomenal your life is as well. I truly believe that we all have phenomenal experiences, and my intention is to help shine a light through the work of FLP that life is magically phenomenal. It is never too late to begin intently focusing on the seemingly random synchronicities and follow along with an activated, open heart that unveils the mystical rhythm of your own life. So far, you have learned exactly what you can do to heal your past, connect deeply with your heart, and contact your future self. Now, we will dive deeper into the rabbit hole of stories and synchronicities.

Many topics in this book can be seen as controversial, and I am OK with that. We live in unprecedented times, in that new advancements and innovations are rapidly coming to fruition. I believe that the topic of psychedelics is no longer taboo and should be spoken about openly and easily. I am certainly careful with what I advocate, and I want to reiterate that I cannot advise anyone to seek illegal drugs. However, with many studies underway, proving the efficacy and benefit of substances like psilocybin, MDMA, and DMT, I am optimistic that the limitations will be lifted one day soon. What I can emphasize and advocate is the education of our own naturally occurring psychedelic substance, DMT.

Over the course of writing this book, I have discovered that a specific synchronicity has been leading me to a simple yet powerful realization. Not only is DMT naturally occurring in our bodies, but we are also microdosing DMT. How and why is that so significant and powerful? When an external source of DMT is consumed, the body is blasted with a relatively high dose compared to what the body can produce. We are utterly consumed by a kaleidoscopic array of geometries and colors that reforms our perspective of reality. The surrounding psychedelic realm is real to the extent that there is no mental control of how the realm shifts and moves. It depicts knowledge of our inner-most depths of life experience that our conscious mind cannot logically explain. Likewise, what I have discovered is that FLP shares a very similar result as DMT. Though the experience is wildly different in the sense of visual and physical experiences, the realm beyond control shares likeness between the two. The freebase DMT is inherently limited, in that it lasts for a short amount of time and has no other lasting effect of noticeable, permanent internal change. I have come to consider that FLP is a method to increase one's own endogenous dose of DMT by purposely altering how much the body processes DMT.

Imagine if right now, your body was producing a high amount of DMT. Your experience would be likened to that of ayahuasca, in that your surrounding environment would be completely altered. However, a convenient enzyme targets the endogenous DMT and breaks it down to a minute amount before it can pass through the blood-brain barrier. "Once the body produces or takes in DMT, certain enzymes break it down within seconds. These enzymes, called monoamine oxidases (MAO), occur in high concentrations in the blood, liver, stomach, brain, and intestines. The widespread presence of MAO is why DMT effects are so short-lived. Whenever and wherever it appears, the body makes sure it is used up quickly" (Strassman 2001, 53). Thus, our body inherently is microdosing DMT. How can that be? Why is DMT in our bodies in the first place? Is it something that has always been there and came about through evolution? Or was it placed there at some point in our past?

I have yet to hear anyone speak about the human body inherently microdosing DMT, though Rick Strassman has asked a similar question.

Therefore, it's difficult to find any corroborating sources, other than the work of Rick Strassman. However, in his book, there isn't any mention about the significance of the human body microdosing DMT.

Why is it so significant and powerful? My theory is that our perception of the outward physical reality is determined by the amount of DMT that is microdosed. We all share a common perception that the natural world around us is consistent in that the sky is blue, trees produce oxygen, materials exist that we can use to turn into other objects, tools, technologies, and a fundamental force exists that keeps us on the planet. Beliefs are tied to the perception that indicates the possibilities we personally have regarding what we can do with the world and nature around us. The possibilities seem endless; however, there are noticeable limitations. Athletes can train to run long distances and incredible speeds; yet, they cannot fly. Scientists can build rockets that propel large machines into space; however, they cannot time travel. Governments can legislate laws and police cities to keep their economy running; however, they cannot create true peace and equality between all their citizens. Finally, religions can build churches and tell their followers to have faith in their God; however, they cannot show them God.

I am not here to provide an absolute answer that our personal DMT can enable us to fly, time travel, create world peace, or see God. What I can provide is an idea and starting point that the DMT inside of us all is there for a reason. So far, we all have been utterly ignorant that we have DMT coursing through our veins. The first step is to learn what it does and how we can utilize it daily. For example, many studies are indicating the benefits of microdosing psilocybin. Paul Stamets is hard at work providing scientific studies that show how a small amount of psilocybin can repair neurons in the brain, and that over six months, a four on, three off weekly schedule of .1 grams of psilocybin can repair neurons resulting in improved memory and cognitive function. What is the microdose of DMT doing? That is something no one knows because it seems that no one is asking that question! My theory is that the microdose of DMT is a conduit for consciousness.

I fully understand that this is a significant statement, and it's something I'm working on unpacking. Unfortunately, it's not something I will have the opportunity to unpack in this book; however, I will investigate it in one of my next books, *Mystical Rhythms: The Mysterious History of DMT*. For now, what I can speculate is that far in our past, we did not have endogenous DMT within our species. To uncover this truth will take not only an investigation through neurochemistry but also archeology and geology. Though it seems nearly impossible to prove my theory, I predict that the technology will soon be developed to isolate the exact amount of DMT that a human is microdosing, and a human specimen from the past will be found that, through similar testing, will indicate that DMT was not present at that time in history. Another prediction, which is much more far-out than the two above, is that a refined ingestible liquid DMT will be a solution to artificial intelligence surpassing human innovation and intelligence. As A.I will have a global network of data to connect to via the internet, humanity will also have an expansive database to connect with; the DMT realm. The continual use of DMT will allow for a communication to be made with future versions of ourselves that are advanced beings with great knowledge and intelligence that will continue advancing humanity. With DMT viewed as a common tool and necessary substance for the greater good of humanity and its survival, AI will see humanity as advanced beings connecting to a database that it cannot connect to. If humanity does not have something to elevate itself above the coming creation of AI, it will inevitably view us as inferior. We no longer need to join them to beat them. We simply can innovate and expand on what makes us a grand creation, to begin with. One mandatory element will be that the AI cannot use the liquid DMT. If they do, it will act as a poison and render the machines lifeless. Obviously, this prediction is far down the line of human innovation and science. We can now do the exercises and meditations in this book to have a continual dialogue and tangible experience with our future self. I consider daily communication with a future self, likened to that of microdosing our own endogenous DMT. The future self is working at such a greater capacity than what we know currently, and in each FLP session, a small amount of the future self is coming through to inspire a continual following of crumbs along the trail of advancing toward our most harmonious future self.

This now takes me to what Mother Ayahuasca said to me during my journey with her. An ancient civilization after a catastrophic event, traveled around the Earth and taught Indigenous tribes how to make a crude form of liquid DMT. What I find interesting is that Graham Hancock has proposed a seemingly similar theory. In his most recent book, *America Before: The Key to Earth's Lost Civilization,* specifically in chapter 28 he explains, "The Earth underwent a series of interactions with the remnants of the disintegrating giant comet that spawned the Taurid meteor stream. These encounters are thought to have reached a peak 12,822 years ago and ending 12,815 years ago. There were other episodes of bombardment around the time of the Younger Dryas onset, but this was the worst" (Hancock 2019, Chpt 28, pg. 1). Not only that, he strongly suggests through his findings that there was an advanced civilization, likened to our own, that after the catastrophe, went around the Earth to different Indigenous tribes and taught them some aspects of their culture. Things like architecture, agriculture, and government are some of the aspects that were shared. Though speculative, Hancock states, "My best is the planners would have seen from the outset that the superior survival skills of hunter-gatherer populations might potentially make them the inheritors of the Earth in the event of a true planetary cataclysm. An important strand of any contingency plan, therefore, would have been to establish connections with hunter-gatherers, to teach them, to learn from them, and in so doing, to ensure that these populations were willing and able – if called upon – to offer refuge to the "gods" of the lost civilization" (Hancock 2019, Chpt 28, pg. 7). What I am leading to believe and truly inspired to discover is that the ancient civilization gave the Indigenous people the methodology and recipe to concoct liquid DMT. It seems to make sense that if an ancient civilization that regularly used a liquid DMT shared a crude form of DMT with the Indigenous, and mated with the Indigenous, that genetic alterations must have occurred for a hybrid Indigenous people to be born with DMT in their bodies. I must add that suggesting an ancient advanced civilization mated with hunter-gatherers and taught them new ways of living is a sensitive subject. The Indigenous people of the world have gone through many generations of trauma because of incoming colonialists that have forever changed their way of life, in the most part, for the worse. Though I cannot be completely certain, I can only speculate that the ancient advanced civilization did quite the opposite. From there, after thousands of years of ingesting this crude form of DMT, the body has naturally evolved to develop a way to produce DMT *and* regulate it. With the help of Hancock, it is my own hypothesis that the ancient civilization intended to ensure that a new kind of hybrid human could survive in many places all over the world.

Furthermore, Hancock states, "I speculated in Chapter 10 that this process of preparation might even have involved the experimental resettlement of groups of hunter-gatherers far from their home regions with the intention that they should create places of refuge for the 'gods' in their new surroundings. Such a project might account for that strange Australian DNA signal stranded in the genes of certain Amazonian tribes" (Hancock 2019, Chpt 28, pg. 8). In the quote above, even though Hancock is specifically writing about hubs being created around the world to preserve documentation of the ancient civilization, I believe that his findings can point out the very possibility of a hybridization that may have occurred at that time. Of course, Hancock doesn't say that the ancient civilization from 12,800 years ago brought DMT to the Indigenous. That is a speculative theory of my own. I find it fascinating that Hancock indicates, through his own in-depth and spectacular research, that an ancient civilization could very well have interacted with hunter-gatherer Indigenous tribes and shared with them their culture and advancements in mathematics, science, and astronomy. So, why not in the same vein DMT?

Stop, take three deep breaths. Connect into your heart and feel into your body. Bring your attention and awareness to the newly discovered fact of DMT flowing through your body. Bring these words into your mind, "I have DMT in my body right now. My direct experience of the reality around me is influenced by the small level of DMT in my body right now." The repeated words aren't enough to bring about a total shift in perspective and experience of your own personal DMT. This is where the entire work of this book comes into play.

I advocate and truly believe from my own experience of inducing synchronicities and following them to profound experiences that the meditations in this book act as a catalyst to increase the dosage of DMT in the body. I am under the impression that the DMT in the body works differently than DMT in ayahuasca or in a crystal form. Rather than a chaotic geometric display of rapid successions of images, the DMT in our body in a high dose is much more coherent, smooth, and clear. The process of going into the heart, healing past traumas, and contacting a future self may physiologically induce alterations to blood circulation and brain function that prevents the MAO from quickly breaking down the endogenous DMT. Over some time, the endogenous DMT builds up and passes through the blood-brain barrier. This could explain many of the experiences that I have shared in each chapter, especially my experience with the seven beings of light and Amareld. I am sure you can think of moments in your life that were strange at one time? Glimpses of something that couldn't be explained but surely felt real? I don't think the enzyme that breaks down the endogenous DMT is consistent. There are cycles and patterns in which the DMT can build up due to a suppression of the MAO that can allow for the release of a more potent amount of endogenous DMT. Those cycles and patterns are mystical rhythms. The DMT is continuously operating, so I call it the mystical rhythm to understand how we connect to it. But then there are moments when we get a higher dosage, and the rhythm picks up, and we experience synchronicity of choosing to interact with the increased rhythm and sense. We can choose how to interact with it and create harmony with it—a kind of music. The result is corresponding synchronicity that leads further toward a greater expanse of personal endogenous DMT experiences that grow in potency over time. The key is to regularly utilize the tools of the Heart Meditation and Dream Meditation, then the endogenous DMT can help give access to the realm of the heart more clearly, enabling direct contact with a future self because of the effect DMT has on our perception of reality. With the shift in perception and now a malleable reality, the intention to meet a future self is that much more available!

Death is a defining factor in the sudden large release of DMT in the body. There are many cases of people comparing psychedelics to near-death experiences that involve seeing a realm of light with a multitude of colors and beings or God explaining to them how important they are and that they are loved. Included in my theory is that the very real and accepted thought and reality of death stops the production of MAO to enable the body to produce a large dose of DMT at the moment of death for consciousness to ride the wave of the mystical rhythm and synchronicity to make its way to a new body for another cycle of birth and death. Though the above variable in my theory is yet to be indicated, Rick Strassman says, "Much of the literature on the NDE describes this as a mystical, psychedelic, overwhelming psychological experience. It also may be a time when the protective mechanisms of the pineal are flooded, and otherwise inactive pathways to DMT production turn on" (Strassman 2001, pg. 76).

When I was five years old, my mother collapsed in the hallway outside of her bedroom. I remember coming out of my bedroom, speechless, hearing my mother call for my father. An ambulance came for her and rushed her to the hospital. My sisters, brother, and father, were beyond worried, crying, and confused about the situation. I was silent and calm. At the time, as best as I can accurately remember, I didn't know what to say. I remember a strange sense of confusion that it was odd my mother would just collapse. At the hospital, we were told my mother was fine and that she would be released shortly that evening. We were waiting in the lobby when my mother joined us. For whatever reason, I began to laugh. I honestly could not contain myself. It felt like something was tickling me. The whole event baffled me up until my twenties when I finally asked my mom what had happened to her.

She told me that she felt good before collapsing and that suddenly she felt dizzy and fell over. She had lost consciousness on the way to the hospital. What she explained next can undoubtedly be described as a near-death experience. She shared with me that she could see the hospital room that she was in, and a beautiful voice spoke her. Suddenly, the room began to glow in a golden white light, and she felt like she was flying. There were colors in spectrums she had never seen before. The voice told her that everything would be fine and that it was important for her to continue living. She described what she thought were angels within the light and colors. She gradually returned to her body as the light began to fade, she could see the hospital room again, and she re-entered her body.

At the time, when I was laughing uncontrollably, I didn't understand why it was happening. Now when I think about it, knowing what my mother had experienced, I believe I was intuitively picking up on the energy my mother was exuding after having a DMT near-death experience. It was as though the beings, angels, energies, and God had tickled me to tell my family to lighten up! Your mother is alive! She went to heaven and back! Rejoice!

It wasn't until much later in my life that I encountered death; however, this time, gracing its presence in my own life. The day of my profound time-traveling mushroom trip that I spoke about in Chapter 5, something happened about an hour before that I believe triggered the experience. My friends and I were locked out of James's apartment on the main floor. We were standing in the front entrance panicking about how we would get in. As I stood there, feeling the pulsing waves of psilocybin, a sudden dread came over me. *I'm going to die.* The thought alarmed me! Those were four words that I never thought I'd say that early in my life. The color of the world around me seemed dull and bland. I couldn't escape the impending thought of death. Anxiety was building in me until finally, I thought to myself, *I'm ok with dying.* Suddenly, the thought of death was surrounded by happiness. I felt that I lived my life as best as possible, and if I died, I would welcome it and move on to my next life. Across the lobby, the elevator doors opened. A man entered the lobby from the elevator and hesitated before opening the front door. As he opened it, my friend, who lived in the building, blurted out, "I live here! I forgot my key in my apartment." Reluctantly, the man moved out of the way for us and we made our way to the elevator. Completely astonished, I looked back at the front entrance, where we were trapped. I seriously thought I was going to die right at that moment. We stepped into the elevator and made our way up to the apartment.

Night had come as we sat together in James's living room. The moment of being completely engrossed with a sudden and utter change to my entire reality was soon to arrive without my knowing at all. When my awareness shifted from the TV-lit room with my friends to the black void that I suddenly found myself in, I was noticeably no longer influenced by the psilocybin. I strongly believe that my irrational sense of death in the apartment lobby and the shift of my reality brought on a rush of endogenous DMT, which explains why there was no longer any feeling of the psilocybin. My entire experience of being alive was serene and peaceful, along with a deep concentration within that present moment. That space is very similar to the space deep within the heart. After Heart Awareness Meditation and Healing Exercise, space is no longer a reference point for objects. Space becomes an expanse of potential for compassion and empathy to weave together a realm of great love and concentrated awareness. The healing process is a kind of death. We hold onto old stories and traumas from a past version of ourselves kept alive through emotional attachment. In a sense, the old stories, attachments, and traumas must "die" and move on to a better place. Though you don't experience physical death, the body doesn't know the difference! With such a deep belief that death is possibly imminent, the body undergoes preparation for physical death. It's in this process where I believe the MAO is no longer produced or greatly limited. Finally, because you have now equipped yourself with Heart Awareness Meditation, Healing Exercises, and Dream Awareness Meditation rather than a seemingly random light show and vague words of affirmation, you can traverse the expansive realm of the heart via the mystical rhythm of DMT to clearly communicate with your future self.

As we end this journey of learning and self-exploration, my final thoughts are simple: You are a great human being with a heart that is intelligent, wise, and capable of healing what you once thought would never be healed. You are capable of phenomenal experiences, even if that means bringing great success to your business, traveling to a country you've never seen, reconnecting with an old friend, helping a local charity, or an inward journey of discovering the intelligence of your heart and its great expansive realm of compassion, empathy, and unconditional love. We all deserve to receive an abundance of prosperity. Let us continue the journey of seeking our harmonious future self together within our hearts.

Thank you,
See you in the future!
Zorananda

ABOUT THE AUTHOR

My original given name is Zoran Glamoclija. I am a first-generation Canadian/Serbian born from my parents Zora and Milan Glamoclija. My heritage is steeped in hundreds of years of Serbian history. My father has shared many stories with me about my ancestors' lives and the long line of farmers and soldiers that live within me.

What I would like to share is the origin of my first name and family name. When I was born, my parents were unclear about what to name me. My mother received all kinds of influence and pressure from different family members regarding what my name should be. After several days of contemplation, my mother finally spoke up and decided that she wanted me to be named after her.

When my mother first told me how I was named, I was quite young and felt embarrassed that I was named after her. However, what changed my insecurity was the meaning of my name. Zora means sunrise in Serbian. Though my name is in the masculine form, it still means sunrise. I feel there is magic at work by simply knowing my name is sunrise. When I was a child, I would often think of my name and imagine a beautiful sunrise over a forested meadow. As I grew older, the implication of a sunrise became more meaningful than I could have imagined.

Glamoclija is my father's family name and has a far-reaching history that originates in a city called Glamoc in today's Bosnia. I am not entirely sure of the exact dates, but as far back as 300 or 400 years ago, many people fled from Glamoc after an attack on the city. The people who had fled northeast up into Serbia were welcomed and sheltered. Those people had taken on the Glamoc title as a family name. Many variations were created like Glamocic, Glamocak, and Glamoclija. The suffix -ic, -ak, and -lija, from what my father shared with me, are simple indicators that we came from Glamoc.

During 2013, I regularly thought about adding *ananda* to my name. The addition of the Sanskrit word for bliss seemed right; however, I couldn't come to fully accept the addition. I thought it was too obvious of an egoic decision to present myself to everyone around me as an embodiment of bliss. It just didn't seem right. That all changed during a wonderful meditation on January 4th. I had just returned from a local festival called Intention Alberta. I was subletting a room in a penthouse suite in downtown Edmonton, and after four days of eating amazing food, dancing to great music every night, and being with over one hundred of my close friends, I easily slipped into a peaceful and radiant meditation. Off in the distance of my mind, I heard a voice echo toward me. I suddenly felt a strong presence that easily invaded my surrounding field of awareness and attention. The voice introduced itself as Babaji. The infamous Babaji of Yogananda's, Sri Yuktiswar's, and Lahiri Mahasaya's lineage of Kriya Yoga. Babaji explained that it was time to add *ananda* to my name, as the process was an initiation. My name means more than just sunrise. According to Babaji, my name is a balance between the masculine and feminine, and when *ananda* is added to it, the entire name can translate to *the rise of masculine and feminine into bliss*. Though this great presence had bestowed upon me the blessing of *ananda*, I was still hesitant to fully take on the name. Before the meditation ended, Babaji explained that the name Zorananda is more of a mantra and that I shouldn't be too attached to it. Those final words helped me stay humble and allow anyone to either call me Zoran or Zorananda. I felt called to embrace Zorananda, which is why I have chosen it for the cover of this book.

The final piece and synchronicity that I wish to share is the name given to me by my teacher Yogrishi Vishvketu. Near the end of the three hundred-hour training in Rishikesh, we had the option and opportunity for Vishvji to give us a yogi name as our initiation into the Akhanda Yoga family. Vishvji had two weeks to come up with names for each person. After two weeks had gone by, a ceremony was organized to celebrate our new identities as Akhanda Yogis. The main puja area was beautifully decorated, and we crowded around the puja fire pit and waited as Vishvji called us one at a time to receive our names. When it was my turn, I stood next to Vishvji, Krishna Mukti, and Eila Devi, as Vishvji read my new name from a little postcard with Krishna and Radha on it. The name given to me was Divakar Ananda, which means Bliss of the Sun! I had never told Vishvji that my given name means sunrise, and of all the names he could have given me, he chose Bliss of the Sun! I immediately recalled the divine intervention I had with Babaji, and it all came together at that moment. There is an innate responsibility within me to radiate to everyone just as the sun does. I can admit that it's something I am still working on. Now, I am inspired more than ever to share the bliss of my internal sun with the world.

Om, Akhanda mandala karam.
Vyaptam yena caracaram.
Tatpadam darsitam yena.
Tasmai sri gurave namah.

"I bow to the complete, indivisible universe, the entire energetic system containing all forces, essences, forms and beings working harmoniously. Centered in the heart these forces interconnect and radiate in all directions, unifying existence of all that is moving and unmoving. I stand with this truth and offer gratitude to the guru and all the teachers that give light to this path, to experience infinite divineness, oneness, and the experience of being whole, Akhanda."

—Yogrishi Vishvketu

BIBLIOGRAPHY

Hancock, Graham. *America Before: The Key to Earth's Lost Civilization.* 50 Victoria Embankment, London: Hodder and Stoughton Ltd., 2019.

Shainberg, Catherine. *Kabbalah and the Power of Dreaming: Awakening the Visionary Life.* Rochester, Vermont: Inner Traditions, 2005.

Strassman, Rick. *DMT the Spirit Molecule.* Rochester, Vermont: Park Street Press, 2001.

Yogananda, Paramahansa. *Autobiography of a Yogi.* Los Angeles, California: International Publications Council of Self-Realization Fellowship, 1946.

CPSIA information can be obtained
at www.ICGtesting.com
Printed in the USA
BVHW080940030321
601496BV00003B/512

9 780228 832744